Sure Fail

SURE FAIL

The Art of Mismanagement

by Raymond Dreyfack

William Morrow and Company, Inc.
New York   1976

Printed in the United States of America.

1   2   3   4   5   80   79   78   77   76

Library of Congress Cataloging in Publication Data

Dreyfack, Raymond (date)
    Sure fail.

    1. Personnel management.   I. Title.
HF5549.D73   658.3   76-10374
ISBN 0-688-03067-X

to my daughter, Madelaine

Foreword

The brainpower and creative potential of American enterprise has been demonstrated repeatedly. We have conquered space, produced wonder drugs, developed highly sophisticated electronic tools, and accomplished other miracles of science and technology. In doing so we have overcome mind-boggling complexities of research, production, and logistics. But often, when it comes to the simple needs and wants of people, we do not know, or are blind to, what turns people on and off. Instead of inspiring men and women to excel, we embitter them. We convert enthusiasm into apathy or worse.

I agree with Alfred de Musset that "perfection does not exist." But the lengths we go to prove it seem, at times, barely short of incredible. It has worried me for years. While being managed and managing, while serving as a writer-consultant called in on scores of corporate and noncorporate stories, programs, and projects, as an observer from both the inside and outside, I have seen, on the one hand, a fair share of dedication and brilliance inspired by lofty intentions and dreams. This was balanced, on the other hand, by blunders and bloopers, some of gargantuan proportion. I'm not referring to the simple, honest errors we all make because we're human. I'm talking about the wasteful, shameful, and entirely unnecessary blunders of style, philosophy, and politics that gnaw away at ideas, corrode profit objectives, and rankle human emotions.

In researching this book I interviewed dozens of executives, supervisors, management consultants, and men and women on the line. Many have their own private horror tales to tell, and bitter memories to purge from their systems. What it boils down to, I believe, is a unique and interesting perspective on the complicated anatomy of profit and nonprofit enterprise.

The organizational thrust these days is toward more productivity—more mileage per person, more return on the buck, increased output per dollar invested instead of higher selling prices. An endless number of techniques and programs have been dreamed up with this objective in mind. But in my experience simply treating people like people will outperform every scheme ever devised for boosting output per person and will help avoid blunders that result in profit erosion.

I disagree with the premise that the best way to learn is through the mistakes that you make. True, mistakes clearly are learning experiences, but making mistakes is the *second* best way to learn. The best way is by studying the mistakes that the other guy makes. Learning through your own mistakes instead of other peoples' mistakes is like going to college as an eligible veteran under the GI Bill of Rights and paying your own tuition.

Sure Fail has been written for supervisors and would-be supervisors, managers and would-be managers, executives and would-be executives, students of human nature and management, and men and women who would like to run organizations instead of running them down. It is a book for anyone who works for a living or expects to do so.

Sure Fail is an early warning system. As my own experience testifies, when you are alerted to managerial pitfalls, it is easier to avoid them.

Contents

CHAPTER 1

Glorification of the "Heavy"

Division X is in a mess after fifteen months in the red, with no sign of recovery. Sales are slipping, customers are deserting, and morale is horrendous. Financial analysts wince when the division is mentioned. On top of that the payroll is overstuffed to the hilt.

Obviously drastic action must be taken, and soon. If this route is traveled much longer, the entire works will be sloshed down the drain. So out of another division you pull John Cool, a promising plant manager who is tougher than rail spikes, and you make him an offer that whips his fervor to a peak.

"Turn Division X around," you tell Cool, "and the presidency's yours."

It is Cool's lifelong dream. Jaw set hard, he jets out to the ailing operation in Frog's Gully, Montana, and assesses the situation. Swiftly spotting the problem, he snaps into action, streamlines systems, eliminates marginal programs, fortifies communications—and the heads roll like bowling balls.

("It's an initiative that should have been taken months ago," one insider admitted to a Wall Street Journal *reporter.)*

Sound familiar? It should. Operation Turnaround is a

perennial favorite of business press editors. A month rarely passes without one or more such stories being featured. Nor is it all PR puffery. Companies do get turned around by courageous, pragmatic managers, but the rampaging cost cutters sometimes destroy the organizations they've been recruited to save.

In a New England multiplant manufacturing company a division's profits kept shrinking in direct ratio to its continuously increasing sales volume. No one could explain why this was happening. The situation persisted over a period of several months. The head man at headquarters finally handed down a mandate: "Either pinpoint the problem and turn the operation around or shut down the plant!"

A bright young problem solver was dispatched to the scene armed with hatchet and scythe. Ambitious and resolute, he reviewed the situation. In less than a week the cause of the deterioration became clear to him, or so he believed. It was a sloppy operation, with standards ignored or unset. Errors proliferated like moisture-fed fungus. Absenteeism and lateness exceeded industry records. To have stated that morale was low would have been to admit it existed.

Horatio J. Plantsaver set his mind to the task. He saw what had to be done. Employees in this plant were getting away with mayhem. The payroll was laden with fat. The operation was as loose and undisciplined as an unbridled filly. What the division needed was a strong, steady hand and a head focused on profits.

Plantsaver's first strategy was to sift through the records and fire 10 percent of the division's least-productive workers. If this didn't get the message across to the rest, he reasoned, nothing would. Within hours pure chaos erupted. Mass sitdowns occurred at all levels, followed by stealing and sabotage. In two months' time the plant's doors were shut, but not before a high-priced consultant was flown in to see what, if anything, he could salvage. He didn't find much. But what he found made him shudder: a history of poor labor relations and worse supervision, ineffective communication regarding work objectives and performance, and unfair treatment of employees. When Plantsaver peered into the powder keg, it had been on the verge of exploding. So he blithely lit the fuse.

Clearly, as the consultant pointed out, priority number one should have been the human-relations job of restoring management's credibility, good faith, and rapport. The indiscriminate slashing of heads is a surefire route to Sure Fail. When the heavy is mindlessly given free rein, he tends to assume deific powers as his natural right.

The hard-nosed Cagney type of executive often emerges as a kind of national business hero—he is glorified in the press, his single-minded purpose extolled. When profits sag, tearing through an operation with ax blades flashing is regarded by many as the realistic and practical course of action to take. But press reports can be misleading. When the indiscriminate hatchet man wields his blade without caution, some good blood is apt to get spilled along with the bad.

Corporations most certainly are obliged to shore up profits, keep shareholders happy, restore analysts' confidence, increase the return on that shriveling investment dollar, and set the stage for survival. No one would advocate disregarding practical considerations or sidestepping actions that have to be taken. The quarrel here concerns head chopping and program curtailment where human feelings and responses are inadequately considered—and the consequences ignored.

You must have heard the pronouncement a hundred times or more, "A manager's job isn't a popularity contest." Yet the superior you genuinely like and respect is the one you'll put out for, not the corporate tough who kicks you in the groin.

Obviously the corporation president who declares Arbor Day a company holiday because it will gladden the hearts of his employees probably won't be around very long.

Nothing could be more suicidal than giving away corporate assets beyond what is practical and in keeping with competitive practice.

But however justified a cost-cutting program may be —and regardless of whether you call it cost reduction or profit improvement—if you conduct it in a manner that is oblivious to the reactions of your people, it will almost inevitably backfire. In a St. Louis sports equipment company a consultant was hired to gauge productivity. His finding was about a 52 percent performance rating in contrast with the 75 percent he claimed was attainable.

What can we do about it? management wanted to know.

The consultant laid out a program. One problem, he explained, was the way desks in the office were arranged. Set up in blocks of four, clerical employees sat side by side, facing each other. The unceasing dialogue was inevitable. The result was a minimum of output and excessive errors due to failure to concentrate on work.

The reasoning made sense to the company's top brass. In one bold stroke the office was revamped. Employees were separated, so that chatter became difficult. It seemed to be a simple solution to a simple problem. It was anything but that. Chaos broke out. The staff was choleric. Absenteeism rocketed. Some people resigned indignantly; others deliberately stalled. After only two weeks the original layout was restored.

Does this imply that management should have ignored a situation in obvious need of attention? Not at all—the same office rearrangement would have worked had it been made more discreetly over an extended period of time, ideally with the invited participation of the people affected. A few desks could have been moved one week, others later; a gradual shifting would have avoided the jolting shock of change and the direct implication that employees couldn't be trusted. Clearly had the changeover been handled more tactfully and diplomatically, the clerical force would not have felt put down.

A good basic axiom to keep in mind in order to avoid supervisory fumblings is: "No one enjoys losing face."

Or take another situation that happened in a Philadelphia warehousing company. With virtually no prior notice fifty-five workers were lopped from the payroll and replaced by automatic lifting equipment. Economically, organizationally, and from a pure financial business standpoint the move made sense. But the timing did not. The climate, already charged with labor tension, had been ripe for explosion when the layoff was announced.

In retaliation, notes one executive, "Workers beat hell out of the trucks, so that maintenance zoomed."

It cost the company more than $70,000 to reinstall the old system and then launch another new program to phase in the automatic equipment.

As innumerable case histories bear out, such dramas starring corporate executioners are commonplace on the stages of public and private enterprise. Whether the impulsive and insensitive treatment of people takes the form of indiscriminate head chopping or jolting change that produces psychological shock, employee response is too often the same: the kind of bitterness, resentment, and defiance that cripples productivity and defeats profit objectives.

CHAPTER 2

The Emperor Waltz

Some managers, with Napoleonic self-indulgence, get carried away by their own magnificence. If such a person happens to run an organization, a division, or even a department, he can smother the talents and stunt the growth of the people who work for him.

A man comes to mind who is chairman, principal stockholder, and supreme reigning mogul of a medium-size plastics-producing operation, with headquarters in New York and two manufacturing plants in the area. Once each week His Royal and Exalted Highness visits each of the plants.

Now this particular monarch does not wear a crown. Nor is he attended by squires and footmen. But the effect is the same. So far as that operation is concerned, he functions like a Caesar or a Nero.

He arrives in a chauffeur-driven limousine, which pulls into the number one parking space by the entrance. The chauffeur scrambles out to throw open the door, then races ahead to the plant's front door. Inside the lobby the royal eyes move critically from object to object. Once, it is said, he spied a cigarette butt on the floor and pointed this out to no less an executive than the division president. Since that time, on the day the supreme commander is due, the plant is as spotless as a Marine barracks awaiting the general's white glove inspection.

Inside the plant proper His Majesty moves with quiet dignity to a handsome private office that's kept locked the rest of the week. A passing employee greets him with a nervously reverent, "Good morning, sir." He graciously responds.

Word of his arrival has naturally preceded him. The division head's secretary waits by his office to unlock the door for him and fulfill any small request he might have. He acknowledges her greeting with a faint regal smile. Entering the throne room, he seats himself at the head of the sixteen-foot conference table. Within minutes a procession of his top executives file somberly into the room, taking their places at his right and his left by their order of rank.

Each in his turn, the executives review the activities of the week and the progress of programs. If the report is favorable, His Highness nods benignly and moves his eyes to the next man in line. If he's dissatisfied, his criticism is softly sarcastic.

He has never been known to raise his voice or betray any sign of emotion. Nor has he ever been known to light his own cigarette. He merely puts it to his lips and waits a split second. His top aides address him as "Mister" or "Sir."

One former executive was once heard to remark, "If God were in that room, he'd probably expect Him to produce a lighter when needed."

This man has no associates, only subjects who shake and quake in his presence. Despite the high pay, managerial turnover is excessive. The company is in trouble.

Moguls of this type may be an exception today, but variations are by no means uncommon. In his book, *Divorce Corporate Style,* reviewed in *Business Week* by editor-in-chief Lewis Young, publisher Don Gussow recounts his experiences with Cowles Communications, Inc. (CCI). In November, 1966, Gussow's $2.5-million company, Magazines for Industry, merged with the multimillion-dollar publisher of *Look, Family Circle,* and other publications.

Gussow received 101,000 shares of CCI stock, worth about $1.5 million. He was made board director and president of Cowles Business and Professional Publications Division. Having fulfilled a lifelong dream, he says, he was the happiest man in New York.

The dream became a nightmare. As the months passed, Gussow watched the Cowles empire gradually deteriorate under Gardner Cowles's despotic one-man rule. He lists a long rundown of shortsighted moves and incredibly unbusinesslike decisions. When *Family Circle*'s chief competitor strengthened its operation, Cowles failed to respond. The magazine, which had earned $2 million a year before Cowles bought it, lost $2 million a year under Cowles's management.

A rule of thumb in buying newspapers is that the price of the stock should be no more than twenty-five times earnings; Cowles bought the *Ocala Star Banner,* whose stock sold at an unbelievable fifty-five times earnings. He took a $15-million bath on the *Suffolk Sun* and permitted the newspaper to fold. Even after all other big publishers computerized circulation fulfillment operations, Cowles continued paying 2,000 people to do the job by hand. *Look* took an $8-million shellacking in 1970 alone.

By that year Gussow's 101,000 shares had shrunk in value to $350,000. In his book he bitterly accuses Cowles of running a $175-million public corporation as though it were his own private fief, while a bedazed board sat by.

"Unhappily," writes Young in his review, "it is all true—as he saw it." The same dreary deterioration is under way at scores of other companies where the management has lost its zest, its competitiveness, and its will to survive. "*Divorce Corporate Style* is an early warning signal," he adds. It's a "crash course in what happens behind the closed doors of boardrooms where the chairman is king and the directors are courtiers."

In fairness, Napoleonic organization heads who make dim-witted moves and nutcake decisions are probably in the minority. Many autocratic leaders are awesomely brilliant and uniquely creative. A long string of tycoons—from Harriman and Ford to Carnegie and Schwab—could be cited in evidence.

Yet however gifted the czar, undue organizational dependency on one person's judgment and rule can be a shortcut to ruin. One $16-million-a-year manufacturer of industrial products had an autocratic virtuoso at its head who was second to none in the industry. Noted throughout the field for his savvy and instinct, he was a tireless twelve-hour-per-day, six-day-per-week workhorse. Mind, body, and soul were dedicated to his miniature empire.

He was eminently honest and fair in his dealings with people. A benevolent monarch, he was respected by workers and idolized by key aides. His detailed knowledge of operations and problems was uncanny. He was the focus of every important decision, and many secondary decisions as well. His control spanned all major corporate functions—from research and marketing to production and finance. As his devout secretary of some sixteen years put it, "Mr. X doesn't run the company. He *is* the company."

The results were outstanding. Ceded the throne by his father, the founder, he single-handedly tripled sales and profits in a hard, competitive industry. Analysts spoke well of him. No one could fault his business judgment or skill. In the noteworthy years of his reign he made only one serious mistake. It happened on a bright November morning as he walked from his car to his office.

He dropped dead.

It can happen to the best of us. On the heels of The King's demise, a shocked management team stumbled uncertainly into action. The only decisions they had made in the past were deciding when to take problems to the chief. Scared and disoriented, they floundered about like small boys lost at the zoo.

The company headed steadily downhill. It never recovered.

The only truly sound, stable, progressive kind of organization we know is team organization. One-man rule serves to enervate the team.

In California we know of a small service firm that was also chaired by the son of the founder. This fellow wasn't one-fifth the businessman his father had been, and he was shrewd enough to know it.

It didn't faze him particularly. "You don't have to be smart," he said, "so long as you surround yourself with brilliant aides."

It was the old proven philosophy, but sadly misapplied. Instead of surrounding himself with a team of smart managers, he surrounded himself with *one* smart manager.

In the past he had once been in a spot, unable to decide on a matter of major importance. Someone had recommended a management consultant as a "veritable wizard." The prospect of such a man at his disposal appealed to him.

He listened to the consultant and liked what he heard. The advice worked out well. He took to confiding in him regularly. It became a habit in time. He made no important move without his counsel. As it developed, the consultant was soon ruling by proxy.

The arrangement worked well until one unhappy day. The consultant informed him he had been elevated to the presidency of his own firm and would have to relinquish individual accounts. Of course, a top-rated man would be assigned in his place. The young chairman was shaken, and he tried first one replacement, then another. No one worked out. In time he lost confidence in consultants and abandoned their use.

But he was unequipped to act on his own. His people, unaccustomed to making decisions, were unable to help him. They fumbled and blundered. After a year passed, the firm was sold for a fraction of its worth. Whether one-man showmanship is practiced by the ruling monarch in person or by proxy, the ultimate result is often the same. One consequence of the "Emperor Waltz" is that however gracefully the king glides over the floor, his subjects never learn how to dance. Impressive though he may be in his prime, if for whatever reason His Majesty decides to step down from his throne, he will be left with a leaderless kingdom.

CHAPTER 3

Muddled Priorities

Watch your step, please. The desiccated deserts of Blunderland are strewn with the bleached bones of misguided managers who for a variety of reasons persisted in doing the wrong things, in the wrong place, at the wrong time, and wound up lost in the process.

Theoretically in the well-run operation every person has a prescribed function. Each function has associated with it a number of specific tasks and responsibilities. Priorities are ranked by their contribution to the fulfillment of goals.

The muddle-minded manager with priority problems appears to have the pieces of the puzzle turned upside down and backwards and scattered all over the place. He's confused by all the unwritten and ill-defined tasks. He seems uncertain of the relationship between functions and goals and which chores are essential. So he works nonsequentially and starts Act 3 while Act 1—which should have been finished two days ago—is still in progress.

Naturally the show bogs down. From what we've observed, the consequences of Muddled Priorities can be calamitous.

At times they're muddled with the best of intentions. One head of a small-to-medium-size hardware products company almost put himself out of business this way. An avid reader of the management press, he read pronouncement after pronouncement on the importance of people. Competition is people. Quality is people. A corporation's heartbeat is people. He pointed with pride to the excellent human relations in his company. Accessibility personified, his philosophy was "the open door, the open ear, the open mind." But almost anything can be overdone, even kindness to children.

The company got into trouble. One serious problem was its distributor network. Dealers became increasingly dissatisfied over certain merchandising policies. Key customers complained that they were being ignored, that the chief never visited them to talk over their gripes. He was too busy listening to problems at home. Another difficult situation was marginal performance in two satellite plants. The head never got around to reviewing the problem first hand.

The ultimate near-collapse was inevitable. An almost surefire way to turn a routine headache to migraine proportions is to overstress a given priority at the expense of others.

An even more Sure Fail head throbber is to be aware of an overriding priority and pretend that it doesn't exist. Consider what occurred a few years back in a depressed agricultural community in West Virginia. Gaunt, somber-faced farmers in the area were unable to feed their families. Vegetables and potato crops were trundled to market and carted back unsold.

Federal aid was assigned to the area, and officials were designated to set up a poverty program. Quick agreement was reached on what the farmers needed most—a market for their produce. In order to stimulate buying, a Farmers' Market was established. The farmers would bring their crops to market, and the Farmers' Market would buy them. Then the market would take the product and . . . and do what? That was the stickler.

The Farmers' Market was no more able to peddle the stuff than the farmers had been. In a depressed area, of

necessity, most people had planted makeshift gardens of their
own. They would not buy tasteless and inferior produce.
What the Farmers' Market amounted to, in effect, was a
new kind of welfare, a giveaway program.

Of course, that had not been the intention. Though a
nonprofit enterprise, the Farmers' Market was in time supposed to become self-supporting.

Government-appointed experts were flown in to review the situation. When they observed what was happening,
the recommendation was even simpler than the original proposal to set up the market: "Shut it down!" Despite political
protest, the disgruntlement of the farmers, and indictment
by the press the operation was discontinued.

But there's a happy ending to the story. Today, in
place of the Farmers' Market, agricultural experts from a
nearby college are working closely with the farmers. They're
being taught what crops to plant on the tough-yielding soil
and the best way to plant them. The community is still a long
way from affluence, but quality produce is now being farmed.
The crops are being sold, and self-sufficiency appears to be
in sight because at long last priority number one has been
given its rightful precedence over priority number six.

Sometimes priority number six takes precedence over
number one because it's more fun for the myopic driver at
the wheel. Take the case of the meek and mild-mannered
city manager of a medium-size New England community
who kept receiving reports of conflict, tension, and declining
morale in the public works department. Apparently trouble
was simmering. Productivity had been slipping steadily, and
a rash of resignations had occurred over the past six months
or so. Marvin Milquetoast was well aware that the situation
demanded his attention at once. What's more, he had a fair
suspicion that the friction centered around the department
head, who was playing favorites and triggering widespread
resentment.

But dealing with personality problems, particularly

where discipline seems to be in order, is no lark for even the tough-minded manager. Marvin found other managerial pursuits far more pleasant. He kept *intending* to confront the supervisor as he should have done months ago. But whenever he felt duty prodding his conscience he settled the debate raging inside himself with the assurance that he would get to it just as soon as priority six or sixteen was out of the way. As a result the situation progressed from lousy to desperate. In time the department was totally disrupted; its most valuable performers who had not quit were completely demoralized.

In marriage, in business, in life, human actions must be geared to human needs in their proper sequence of urgency. Step one on the organizational scene is to evaluate priorities as they relate to organizational objectives. When undecided as to which need comes first, the trick in each case is to examine the consequences of not acting or deferring action. Often this process alone points the way. Where it doesn't, it may be a matter of conferring with others. For whatever reason, rationalizing the postponement of positive action only serves to complicate problems and cause organizational plans to go awry.

CHAPTER 4

Penny Ante Management

"The prodigal robs his heir," the French moralist Jean de La Bruyère once wrote. "The miser robs himself." He robs his organization as well.

Evidence exists in abundance. A well-known pharmaceutical company reputedly pays employees "in the dark." It traps key personnel into long-term employment with pension plan bait. Managers worth $30,000 a year or more sometimes settle for half the amount because they're afraid to give up accumulated pension credits. They trade a viable prime of life for old-age security.

This may seem like a clever way to control talented people. But it often backfires, and in such an operation true loyalty rarely exists. Bitterness and resentment simmer in men and women who are afraid to make the break. They wind up hating themselves for their gutlessness, and hating the company even more.

One research chemist, overworked and underpaid, has developed his own technique for balancing the scale. An experienced professional, he performs his job competently enough. But now and again he comes up with a bright new discovery, an exciting new product idea. When this happens he's ready. He has a deal all set up with a competing drug manufacturer who is happy to purchase his thoughts for a price. The chemist considers the price as an "equalizer" between the compensation he receives and the income he feels he's entitled to.

The managing partner of a New York consulting firm frequently runs into dollar-dumb, penny-wise practices and counsels vehemently against them. "But you should see his own shop," a bitter ex-associate confides. "He counts the paper clips. His ego is as large as his pay scale is small. He sees himself as the supermanager who rewards through exposure, keeping subordinates faithful by sheer force of his magnetism."

The pet theory of this penny ante consultant is the belief that money ranks low on the list of human motivators. He's fond of quoting Ben Franklin's admonition that "a small leak will sink a great ship." In the meantime his own boat is foundering. In twenty years he's been unable to put together a stable executive team. Blinded by greed and self-adulation, this dollar-duped chiseler exists in a fantasy world. He has dreamed up a string of phony ersatz sweeteners that he imagines deludes his people into believing they are being royally treated despite their low incomes. He touts these honors as being more precious than dollars.

He's on a first-name basis, for example, with all employees. Key and subkey personnel get invited periodically to his country place for barbecued ribs and a romp in the pool. He listens with the fervor of a dedicated clergyman to employee problems and concerns—as long as they don't involve requests for more money. His philosophy of management is simple, "Boost a person's self-esteem, and he'll forget about his pocketbook."

He deludes only himself. Employees who move on, often leaving damaging organizational gaps in their wake—and there have been a host of these—characteristically refer to him as "that cheap s.o.b." If he could pause for a moment to think about it he might see that his business strategy is shot full of holes. His occupation is to probe, to improve operations, but investigation stops at his own front door. He's a fake to himself no less than to others. A professionally executed management audit of his firm would quickly reveal that the underpinnings have all but rotted away. Mediocrities stay on, embittered by the humiliation of having to do so but at a loss to do better. Talented young consultants in training, after acquiring the needed experience, move on to fairer rewards and riper pickings. What this man runs, in effect, is a training facility for the competition.

Penny-pinching tactics can produce devastating consequences. In a large mining and manufacturing company key employees went into business for themselves on the side because they were overworked and underpaid. They worked out intricate schemes to flush precious metals down drains, recover them in a nearby dammed-up stream, and peddle them to fences. Supervisors set up assaying operations on their own, using company facilities and personnel. One manager tripled his income by selling company products and supplies. Another set up shop as a consultant, devoting more time to his private practice than to company business. The whole mess was eventually uncovered by an investigative firm, but the losses incurred left the company reeling.

Tight fiscal management frequently is not concerned with how much money is spent but with how wisely it's spent. An Eastern discount chain plagued by sagging profits recently installed a new operating head. He was known in management circles as a rampaging cost cutter and turnaround man. His turnaround tactics were so effective they almost produced a spin. Objective number one was "to trim fat from the payroll and eliminate waste." He made an early pronouncement to prove he meant business, "No new pencils issued unless the stub of the old one is turned in." The edict produced dramatic results. Seventy-two dollars was saved in six months on pencils alone. But morale dropped dead on the heels of the mandate.

A consulting analyst estimated that "the move probably cost thousands of dollars."

Needless to say, it's easier to save money than to spend it prudently. A Pittsburgh-based corporation is multinational, prestigious, and tightly controlled. Managers are hog-tied by their budgets.

"Three years ago," one then-new department head recalls, "I requisitioned a piece of equipment designed to cut certain clerical costs by a third and save thousands of dollars."

No "blue sky" was contained in the estimate. It was hard-nosed and practical. Procedures were spelled out in detail, savings documented to the very last nickel. The plan was irrefutably foolproof.

Yet the proposal bounced back like a Yo-Yo. There was no discussion, no explanation—only a simple rubber-stamped dismissal, *"Requisition exceeds budget!"*

The frustrated manager had worked for weeks on his proposal. He had expected to gain status as a minor hero, at least, as a result of his efforts. Instead, he was squashed like a grape. "It taught me a lesson," he confides. "Never underestimate the sanctity of the budget around this place. The budget is inviolable. It overrides reason and needs."

Since that experience the manager plays budget Parcheesi like some gamblers play blackjack at Vegas. He keeps a cushion of cash in reserve. Since future budgets are in the main based on past expenditures, he overstates current needs to preserve future allocations. At the end of last year, for example, he found himself with $20,000 worth of unspent allowance on hand. To dispose of the money he bought unneeded supplies, hired a team of temporary people to make a study that didn't have to be made, and purchased a porridge of frill items for himself and his assistants.

Other department heads work much the same way. Toward the end of December one marketing manager telephoned a photographer who fulfills free-lance assignments.

"Send me a four-thousand-dollar invoice for services rendered."

"What services?"

"Don't worry about that. Something will come up next year to cover it. Just make sure I get the bill before December thirty-first."

Penny-pinching tactics at their worst are practiced by managers who go through all kinds of involved acrobatics in an effort to impress shareholders regarding current profit performance.

To jazz up its earnings statement one company scalpels the heart out of advertising and promotional programs to show an increase in immediate profits at the expense of future sales and market position. Another automates every semblance of humanity out of secretarial services, thus paring the payroll but undermining morale. A third lowers materials standards, cheapening the product and driving customers to deal with competitors.

Very Kempf, savvy editor of *Plant Engineering,* issues this pragmatic appeal to component buyers, "I wish the National Association of Purchasing Agents would tell me what occult power their members use to determine the value of a component on a purchase requisition. As an example, let's consider a simple limit switch with an acquisition cost ranging from ten dollars to twenty dollars." Faced with a choice between the $10 switch and a superior $20 unit, Kempf says, few purchasing agents could resist buying the less-expensive item and chalking up what appears to be a $10 saving.

"Everyone is happy," he adds,

> except the plant engineer. Why? Because he knows that particular limit switch is to be used on an application where downtime runs ten dollars per minute, limit switches fail frequently, and it usually takes ten to fifteen minutes to find the defective limit switch and replace it. In other words, he could easily justify paying one hundred dollars for a limit switch if one could be found with superior life for this application.

It's not easy to hoodwink your people, even if it were desirable to do so. Someone once said that economy is a way of spending money without getting any pleasure out of it. No matter how the spending squeeze is labeled, to most employees, however you serve it up, it's the same old malarky. It takes more than gung ho pep talks for cost reduction to succeed. First, people must be sold on the goals set forth. Second, they must be made to visualize the rewards involved. Third, and most important, they must be permitted to share in the rewards.

Nor does the sharing allude to glory alone. It refers to take-home pay—dollar diplomacy in the workplace. It refers to using and spending money as a means to an end, not as an end in itself. But most of all it refers to fair and realistic compensation, that is, giving people the wage they deserve as determined by their service, contribution, and effort.

CHAPTER 5

Top-of-the-Headsmanship

As any schoolboy will tell you, if you don't do your homework, you flunk. Someone should tell this to the Sure Fail manager. Bypassing your homework flunks you not only in school but in business as well.

A quip about a top-of-the-headsman once appeared in Winchell's column, "He knows all the answers; it's the questions that confuse him." Too many executives simply don't ask the right questions when faced with decisions and problems. Harvard Professor Myles Mace once reached this conclusion following a survey he conducted. As an illustration of this, consider the Allis-Chalmers (A-C) debacle of the early 1960s. It took plunging profits plus an onslaught of takeover attempts by unwanted suitors to convince the A-C board that some "discerning questions" were called for.

Shortchange your homework today, and you may wind up wearing a dunce cap tomorrow. In the complex deals and transactions encountered in the game of business these days there's only one way to rake in the pot, or at least come out even: that's via deep-probe analysis.

Thomas Hardy wrote in his *Notebook*, "Though a good deal is too strange to be believed, nothing is too strange to have happened."

Financial wizard James J. Ling, who parlayed a lot of chutzpah and a dream into a $1-billion empire, will confirm this with a chuckle. The story is told by Stanley H. Brown in his book entitled *Ling*. One day the conglomerator and his aides met with financial executives of The Prudential Insurance Company to discuss the sale of Ling's computer technology operation. Ling, expecting Ma Pru to offer $60 million to $65 million, decided he would settle—after the obligatory haggling—for $75 million to $80 million.

But "the man from Prudential" popped up with a $90-million offer right out of the box. Suppressing gulps of astonishment, the Ling cadre had to adjourn quickly for a private caucus, lest they tip off their shock and delight at the offer. What it added up to was a $25-million faux pas, one that could not not have occurred had the Pru boys been cracking their books.

When your executive playpen contains large sums of the green, it's important not only that you do your homework but that you do it with painstaking thoroughness. Muck up just one significant detail, and the dollar drain can be devastating. No one knows this better than old Charley Wohlstetter, master builder and corporate chieftain, who is known for his savvy and dealmanship. Wohlstetter once worked out a deal to construct prefab homes in a shut-down Lockheed plant in California. The technology was faultless, but he had failed to bone up on a restrictive local building ordinance that effectively made the transaction impossible. It was a mistake that cost millions. By his own admission, "It was one of my most brilliant failures."

More often, when Johnny neglects doing his homework, he's not prone to admit it. In the dark and dreary late sixties when the ill-fated Penn Central was slowly heading off track, top brass were reluctant to discuss the Great Computer Muddle that was spawned by the Pennsy-New York Central merger. Some industry insiders will tell you that the mix-up was inevitable and that provisions should have been made to properly coordinate communications and make the systems of the two lines compatible.

Both railroads were heavy users of automation. But their setups were as different as snow is from cheese. In a mind-busting mishmash of IBM hardware and software, Friden Flexowriters, teletype inquiry systems, cathode ray graphics, random access disc files, and magnetic tape drives, all whipped together into a psychedelic electronic nightmare, rail cars that were supposed to be in Boston wound up in Sioux City, and shipments that were supposed to be unloaded in Cleveland ended up stranded in Hartford, Connecticut.

Conditions reached a measure of frustration so intense it caused one major shipper to grumble, "They've taken the worst services of the two lines and combined them, and that's what the shipping public is getting today."

With traditional Sure Fail fortitude, top officials disclaimed credit for the fiasco. They contended that since the merger deal had been thrashing through the courts for months, management could not be sure of approval until the very last moment. Under such conditions, how could the expenditure of millions to make the systems compatible be justified?

On the other hand, with total chaos inevitable as a result of inefficient communications in a business where communications is the key to good service, how could the failure to analyze the problem and do the job that had to be done be condoned? It's a question industry experts—and some shareholders, thrown into the wallpaper business when their stock became worthless—are still asking.

What produces such masochistic incompetence among the byways of Blooperville? Perhaps the most obvious cause is sheer laziness. Coasters coast and once-dynamic go-getters tend to wallow in the sunlight of past glories.

There's nothing like the pungent odor of fat profits in the offing to fog up managerial perspectives. Occasionally, like a pup sniffing a hydrant, when the chief at the helm catches what he takes to be the scent of easy bucks to be made, he tosses caution to the wind. Without adequate spade work and study he plunges into deals that become ordeals. In one classic example a New England footwear maker went out of his way to gloat publicly about rocketing sales. The ambitious chief executive of an acquisition-minded mini-conglomerate wooed the shoe maker like a bitch in heat, and worried lest a competitive swain beat him to the quarry. A quick deal was made, the acquisition rapidly consummated. The triumphant suitor strutted for less than a week.

It didn't take long for the financial wizards to learn that the acquired company was losing money faster than its revenues could be deposited. After the acquisition it was disclosed that the shoe company was a sales-hungry operation lacking modern cost controls, management structure, or profit orientation. Worse, it was largely dependent on a single customer, who set his own prices and virtually wrote his own ticket.

Dow Chemical Company's much-publicized decision to produce napalm has been described as one of history's "most idiotic public relations blunders." The original bid to make this devastating bomb ingredient came from the company's Government Affairs Department, and it was based on routine profit considerations. This is less to be faulted, perhaps, than management's final okay of the bid. What followed —student pickets and boycotts, public denunciation by religious and other institutions, and a bad press that lingered for years—is common knowledge to all. Clearly the failure to delve analytically into the inevitable consequences of the decision must rank among the costliest of boners ever made by modern industry.

Another boneheaded decision touched off by the sweet lure of profits is candidly described in *Fortune* by Eberhard Faber, chief executive officer of the writing-products company bearing his name. A clearly superior product called "whiteboard" had been developed in the labs. The writing was easier to read than anything chalked on blackboards. There was less glare and no smudging when erased.

Faber didn't see how the product could miss. It tied right in with the company's regular line sold through school-supply houses and other educational distributors. Schools and colleges would gobble it up.

Faber didn't see because he didn't look hard enough. An all-out program was launched. The product brought nibbles but no signs of gobbling. Had the company probed properly it would have learned in time about a major marketing difficulty it could not have foreseen without careful investigation and analysis. The whiteboard panel was a capital item for schools, which meant an entirely different and more complicated procurement procedure than the one applied to the purchase of pencils and erasers.

Faber explained, "Given the financial crisis that schools generally have been in recently, there just wasn't much heart to take on new lines." The company finally wound up with three alternatives: to sell off the whiteboard line, to liquidate it, or to move production to a plant where it could be manufactured more economically. The decision reached was the last one, the wisest one at the time. But the anticipated whiteboard bonanza simply never developed.

Faber added, "The moral I drew . . . was not to worship the false God of Gross Profit Margin. We now base all our product decisions on models that project to the bottom line."

This is another way of saying, "We analyze to the hilt."

As the evidence shows, even the whiz kids of Blunderland are vulnerable to top-of-the-headsmanship. In fact, the more successful you get, the more vulnerable you become.

This calls to mind the sorrowful saga of a West Coast-based research organization that specializes in market analysis for its clients. Created two decades ago by management engineers and scientists from one of America's most prestigious think tank organizations, the operation took off like a Canaveral-launched rocket. It made scores of acquisitions in the consulting field and was described as an emerging giant with a $10-billion market. Its stock zoomed in 1970 to $53 from an offering price of $7 when it went public in 1964. Management's Midas touch was indisputable.

When it came to market analysis savvy, the firm was second to none in its field. It made just one major blunder. It never did for itself what it did for its clients. The company embarked on an ambitious expansion program into areas outside its competence, with little thought to market demands and requirements. The result was disaster. In 1973 its stock dived to $3 a share. Outside directors and subsidiary chieftains rose up and rebelled. What is more, they took over. Today, the whiz kids are out, and a new top team is in.

The antidote for top-of-the-headsmanship is thorough planning, preparation, and analysis. It's a matter of asking the right questions and getting the right answers in time, *before* committing manpower, resources, and money to programs and projects.

As Francis Bacon once said, "A prudent question is one-half of wisdom." It's the half that Sure Fail managers most often ignore.

CHAPTER 6

Clinging Vine Syndrome

When the corporate commander-in-chief is a one-man band, with the organization his consuming lifetime interest, he's apt to find it's no lark stepping down. If he's a mulish old tyrant and tenacious puppeteer, he's likely to step down under protest if at all and cling to control with every dram of energy he has left, whether officially retired or not.

It happened in the early days at Ford when Henry the First turned over the presidency to son Edsel in 1919. From then until Edsel's death in 1943 Ford senior held no official corporate title. But no one doubted who was running the company—and running it down.

It happened in the well-publicized fiasco at Genesco, where aging W. Maxey Jarman, presumably retired, continued riding herd over his designated successor, son Franklin M., while profits rode steadily downward.

It happened at Rockwell Manufacturing, where eighty-three-year-old Colonel Willard F. Rockwell—though inactive in the company for more than ten years—forced the president to resign.

It has happened at Norton Simon, Texaco, United Air Lines, Consolidated Foods, and scores of other major corporations. In government it happened when Franklin Delano Roosevelt decided to run for a fourth term.

The strong-willed man at the helm doesn't let go easily. When the organizational machinery is inadequate to eject him from the puppeteer's box, the strings can become hopelessly snarled. Misunderstandings increase. Tempers flare. Everything zooms but productivity.

In one small textile company a savvy, experienced manager with an excellent track record was hired by the chairman, a man in his late sixties, who said he was "phasing out," to coordinate and supervise the marketing function, a job long handled by the chief. The manager noted early in the game that for even relatively minor decisions, the chairman's approval was required. It took little time for a confrontation to develop, and even less time for the new man's decision to resign to be formulated.

Management consultant Bridgford Hunt of The Hunt Co. discusses the problem in *Nation's Business*. When a man builds a business himself, he has to know when to relinquish personal control. If he does it too soon, he loses his company. If he waits too long, he kills the management.

Hunt adds:

> In a troubled situation, the sickness becomes worse. A strong boss pulls in the reins to get control, and this produces results. With such evidence that he is doing the right thing, he tightens his personal control further—and kills everyone else's initiative. He is surrounded by shaken men. They can't make decisions; they don't get any practice, and they've lost confidence in themselves. In a company like that, if the boss gets hit by a bus, literally no one is able to take charge.

In one clinger-dominated distributor enterprise where the nominal title of chief had long lost its significance, a frustrated vice president complained, "Nobody knows who will wind up on top. Managers spend more time politicking than minding the store."

In a financial services company plagued by decision paralysis, a weary executive groaned, "What's the point in deciding? If the boss okays it, the old man will beat it down."

You spot clingsmanship mainly in two kinds of operation. One is the mismanaged organization, where the clinger thrives in his glory. Any management consultant who has made the rounds will have his own horror stories to tell about the outfit where communications are bogged down and organizational structure poorly defined, where retirement policy is vague, where promotion and compensation are as apt to be based on whim as on merit. Then there's the founder, or family-dominated, company, where one-man rule has long prevailed. Here King Clinger plays his own music, dances to his own tune, and expects everyone to keep in step—including his unsuccessful successor. ("I've always been on a first-name basis with every employee, and that's the way I want you to operate.")

Whatever the recipe, the symptoms of clingsmanship are fairly universal: rapid turnover, high absenteeism, and poor morale among key employees. Important personnel changes at the top in such organizations do not seem to change policy or the way things are done. Clinging, from what I have seen, would best be confined to lovemaking or ivy.

There is more than one kind of clingsmanship. Almost as deadly, and much more commonplace than top-man tenacity, is middleman tenacity after promotion. This variety of clinging occurs when the climber, having wriggled his way to a higher-level job, finds he's not quite the superman he imagined he was.

Take the marketing executive who was promoted to be an executive vice president of his company, a consumer products manufacturer. For fifteen years this manager had played the key role in planning and organizing his company's trade shows, a job he enjoyed and cherished. Uncertain of his new responsibilities, he continued to enjoy and cherish setting up trade shows after being boosted upstairs. Instead of turning this chore over to the manager who had moved into the marketing slot in his place, he retained it for himself.

The inevitable consequence was neglect of important duties of the executive vice presidency. Problems weren't long in developing. When frictions erupted among certain division heads and department heads and got out of hand, the top man wanted to know why.

When he tried to query his aide, he found him out running a trade show. Investigation revealed the communications and coordination network, presumably controlled by his number two man, was in sad disrepair. Soon the new VP had nothing to cling to, not even the trade shows.

Elsewhere, a Midwestern fabricator of laminated products advanced a maintenance manager to a key operating executive's job. Unsure, insecure, and immature, the guy clung to the things he knew best. In his reports to top management he included maintenance details ranging from light bulb replacement to the performance of various lubricants. When he was informed by his superiors that what was needed was intelligence relating to overhead, personnel, materials, and equipment, he was slow to get the message. Treating the vital information superficially, he continued to overemphasize his old responsibilities, the only ones he could handle with confidence. Unfortunately he soon blew that opportunity as well. He was given the ax after less than five months on the job.

Functional clingsmanship is as chronic an ailment on the organizational scene as dysentery among water-drinking tourists in Mexico. Nor is it confined to middle-management ranks or restricted to commercial enterprise. A hospital executive with a strong computer and financial background and the right friends in the right places was recently eased into a top administrative post. This manager long had concentrated primarily on planning and budgeting, and he continued to focus on these when he took over his new job. The results were predictable. People problems went begging for attention. Existing frictions between key medical and administrative personnel were permitted to heat up into major conflagrations. Internal communications broke down, and community relations deteriorated. The institution, formerly relatively viable, was in deep trouble within six months of the new head man's ascension. Habitually routinized action often tends to deactivate. It's like Aunt Sarah and her rocker. No one ever has to question where Aunt Sarah, well into her eighties, is to be found. She virtually lives in her rocker. Comes meal time she totters off to the table. Comes sleep time she totters to bed. The rest of the time she spends rocking away in a state of perpetual ennui.

The "Rocking Chair Rock" can become a kind of deadly compulsion, enervating and crippling. Considering Aunt Sarah's age and infirmities, she's entitled to do it. But when the old rocking chair is transplanted from parlor to boardroom, it's an invitation for arterial decline to set in. This all too often occurs in the executive chambers of Blunderland, where despite suite talk to the contrary fusty old men at the top prize personal comfort, convenience, and status over organizational progress and growth. Where "Rocking Chair Rock" is the dance of the day, management turns blind eyes to renewal and change. For change implies risk; it implies thought; it implies work—all of which militate against comfort and convenience, the basic tenets of clingsmanship.

For the experienced organizational prober, the "Rocking Chair Rock" is fairly easy to spot. Characterized by do-nothingness, it produces a faint musty odor around executive offices and conference rooms. A classic example involves a leading maker of chemicals, pigments, and dyes. It was no news to analysts in the early seventies that the company's earnings were skidding, labor strife was rampant, management was badly in need of new blood, and its share of market was diminishing gradually.

A point of crisis was reached; irate shareholders pressured for action. The result was that a dynamic management pro and former consultant was brought in as chief executive officer to clean up and thicken the bloodstream. He described what he found to the press, "Offices decorated in 1929 modern, a system of management succession where a sixty-four-year-old took over from a sixty-five-year-old, a board of directors where the average age was sixty-six with some members in their seventies and eighties."

As late as last year he remarked, "Now I know what it means to turn the Queen Mary around."

One good turn deserves another, and the best turn you could do for a clingsman—be he the old captain who won't relinquish the wheel or the middle manager who stubbornly hangs on to former responsibilities—is to show him the effect of his intractability on organizational morale and objectives. The trick here is to replace emotion-based motivations with professional management thinking geared to pre-stated goals. As always, the best proof of the pie lies in the lip-smacking response. In organizations where goal-directed performance overrides individual whims—IBM, General Electric (GE), General Motors (GM), Xerox, Mobil Oil, and Procter & Gamble, to cite a small sampling—managerial effectiveness and good profit performance hold steady over the years. In such organizations would-be clingsmen are automatically thwarted by the system.

CHAPTER 7

Cupidity Stupidity

Ideally the way to make an operation pay is to link, by motivation and fair treatment, the personal aspirations and goals of its people to the organization's objectives. When a manager's real or imagined self-interests are in conflict with his employer's, productivity plummets.

Individual and organizational aims tend to clash for a sickening variety of reasons. One of the most unfortunate of these is greed. "The covetous man is ever in want," Horace wrote. Stretching ethics and morality may seem to work for a while. But in the end it often causes grief and embarrassment to individual and organization alike.

This happened at an Eastern luggage manufacturing company where a factory manager purchased several thousand dollars' worth of specialized tools and equipment each year. For several years he had given the bulk of the business to a supplier whose prices were well above the market average, who offered no quantity discounts despite substantial dollar volume of orders, and who made no special deals. No kickbacks were involved, but from time to time the supplier would wine and dine the manager and his wife at an expensive restaurant, and at Christmas time a case of liquor was invariably delivered to his home. Unwilling to jeopardize these "fringes" the manager had long since stopped checking competitive prices. One day, when a general audit of the operation was made by a management consultant hired for the purpose, the excessive prices were uncovered and the manager was given the gate.

John Ruskin once said, "When a man is wrapped up in himself, he makes a pretty small package." The bigger the job that he holds, the smaller the package he makes. A case in point is the chief executive who solves the corporate relocation problem by moving it near his own community, marina, or golf club as a matter of pure self-indulgence.

According to a *Business Week* "Management Commentary" report the frequency with which this happens is surprising. The report further notes that "J. Roger O'Meara, a research specialist with the Conference Board, reports that thirteen major companies moved from New York City to the suburbs (between 1968 and 1972) and that more than half the relocation sites were influenced by the place of residence of their chief executive officers." A consultant specializing in corporate moves believes this figure applies to the whole spectrum of relocations.

The report cites the chairman of a major oil company who moved his company to the West Coast, within easy commuting distance of his New Mexico ranch. The head of a building products company, a skiing aficionado, relocated in Denver, close to Vail and Aspen. The chief executive of a Midwestern conglomerate promoted a move to the Arizona city where his vacation home was located.

"Blatant selfishness in corporate relocations is not the rule," the report concludes. But anxiety exists that

executives' personal preferences play too great a part in site selection. They cite the rush of New York corporations to Westchester and Fairfield counties, where so many executives live. Says Russell Poylo, president of National Home Settlers, Inc., a relocation service: "People are upset because they think the top six or seven higher-ups have made things a lot more convenient for themselves at the expense of the employees as a whole.

The harsh reality borne out by experience is that self-indulgence and greed usually boomerang with Sure Fail regularity. If we confront decisions and actions purely from a "What's in it for me?" standpoint, disregarding what's in it for others, it leads to results opposed to organizational goals. In the proper operating environment what's good for the team is also good for its members, and the other way around.

In some sad situations, unfortunately, ordinarily well-intentioned managers are coerced into thinking about number one first, last, and foremost. A classic example is the Pennsylvania hardware products company where "good old American competition," in the president's view, is the seasoning that adds tang to the stew. His idea of competition is pitting manager against manager. To the chief it's a game. To the unhappy pawns on the chess board it's a nightmare. A grim atmosphere prevails. Attitudes are understandably protectionist—little wonder, since with a false move you're out on your ear.

Take the PR department. The top man needed an aide for the number two slot. A young female publicity writer was by all odds the ideal choice for the job. Ambitious and smart, she would have filled the slot to perfection. She wasn't even considered. She was too imaginative, too much the status quo challenger, too unpredictable. A "yes man" was selected instead. However inept he could be counted on for political support.

In this same outfit another young comer presented his boss with an imaginative money-saving idea. The executive promised to consider the suggestion. Weeks passed. The young man questioned his boss. He was stalled. Finally, pressed, the aide was told that his idea was good but the timing was wrong. The idea man disagreed. He took his proposal to a competitor and was hired on the spot to put it into effect. His ex-boss had quashed the idea because, on the one hand, he could see no personal gain and, on the other, he viewed the young man as a threat.

One of the most destructive of all self-servers is the credit-stealing, credit-hogging manager. A good example is the personnel director of a large insurance company whose assistant came to him with an idea. The company was in a labor-scarce area at the time, and it was tough to recruit the caliber of people needed to keep the clerical workload up to standard and on schedule. As a result turnover was excessive, and the company paid a premium for office temporaries, who usually lacked the experience required. The assistant's idea was to set up an after-hours shift of workers on a 5 to 9 P.M. basis. The crew would consist of "working mothers" who left the work force to raise families and now wanted to earn money part time.

The manager promised to think the idea over. He didn't have to think for long. His next move was a beeline to his boss's office. "I just came up with an idea and would like your reaction to it." He never bothered to mention his aide.

Some self-serving specialists, sensitive to normal human responses, set up tacit agreements with subordinates that, in effect, state, "Feed me ideas to run with, and I'll take care of you." This is the ancient "one-hand-washes-the-other" axiom. Others don't even bother to maintain this pretense. Either way it's disheartening and frustrating for an individual to come up with a valuable idea or some outstanding achievement and then observe someone else cash in on the recognition and glory. It would be less than human not to react with bitter resentment.

The not-surprising results range from a turnoff of productive ideas to indifference, declining morale, excessive errors, turnover, and sliding performance. Over the long pull the self-server suffers as much as anyone else, perhaps more because he has more at stake. The people he relies upon for loyalty, cooperation, and support wind up as combatants when they might have been allies.

Finally, in a class by himself, is the manager who selfishly serves himself by nursing his ego. This self-centered productivity buster can cost his organization a mint, especially if he's in a position to dip his fingers into the till.

One vain wayfarer who comes to mind is the president of a medium-size consulting firm of thirty-four. When handed the job he thanked his father profusely. Dad, who founded the firm, still makes the important decisions. A team of savvy consultants brings in the bread and upholds the organization's reputation for quality performance. Junior, who in all fairness is a talented salesman, has been given to understand he must steer clear of field operations.

A mod playboy type, his ego is as large as his income. He massages it, to use his own words, by his "contribution to the management literature." This refers to books he's had ghostwritten on how to manage effectively. Although he's had little to do with the content of the books, he has so fallen in love with what has been written in his name that he has persuaded himself he's really the author, and not very subtly proclaims to all and sundry that he is God's gift to management.

One member of the firm wryly observes off the record, "The books are Junior's status symbols. Their PR value is questionable. Their only usefulness so far as I can see is to decorate his office and living room." Unfortunately the tab to get them written and published runs to several thousands of dollars, a heavy drain on the corporate till.

The self-serving manager may suffer from questionable ethics, an oversize ego, narcissistic tendencies, or the uncontrolled desire to hitch a free ride on another man's back. To chomp down on this profit eroder you have to make the penalties for self-service stronger than the real or imagined rewards. By staying targeted on goals and spotlighting actions obstructing them, half the organizational ills could be cured. It takes a watchful eye on the part of the chief and a monitoring system designed to identify deviations from the norm.

As experience proves, the manifestations of self-serving action—low morale, lavish spending on self-indulged frills, chintzy chiseler schemes, projects spawned with personalities and not profits in mind—have a way of revealing themselves when you take the trouble to look for them.

CHAPTER 8

Goldplating

The term "goldplating" was applied by Department of Defense cost cutters during World War II to describe operations that had become swollen with unnecessary frills. "Goldplating" is dispatching a trailer truck when a light pickup will serve as well, or shelling out for a computer when all you need is a calculator, or assigning an $18,000-a-year engineer to do a draftsman's job.

Goldplaters often indulge in excesses when top management is lulled by success. The orders roll in, the goods roll out, and there's extra money to play with. But when times start to harden, surplus cash can dry up faster than dew drops in the desert. This spells trouble and woe for the frills-larded organization. While the freewheeling chief executive blithely dances to the tune of "Hey, Big Spender," his operation winds up paying the piper.

For example, consider the case of U.S. Industries (USI), a trouble-plagued conglomerate founded in 1899 as a rail freight car manufacturer. As World War II was winding down, John Snyder, described by *Fortune* as "a voluble, spellbinding autocrat with a visionary's enthusiasm for large projects," stepped into the driver's seat at USI. He embarked on a diversification program some industry watchers categorized as "misguided." Under his regime cash was dispensed like hot dogs at a ball game, and the economic squeeze of the late sixties caught the company's tail in a vise.

When Snyder died of a cerebral hemorrhage in 1965, financial expert I. John Billera took over the number one spot. A hard-nosed accountant, in retrospect he reveals, "We were just a step ahead of the sheriff." His work, a massive job of salvage and reorganization, was hacked out for him. One of his first acts in office was the thorny task of defrilling the company. He sold off its seven-airplane fleet, its 110-foot yacht, USI's hunting lodge in England, and most of its executive limousines.

"To this day," notes *Fortune,* "Billera has a distaste for corporate 'show'. In spite of the company's expansion, he has restored none of the luxuries. USI is also about as lean as a big company can get. Only ninety-five people work in the corporate headquarters on Park Avenue."

Executive lamentations reverberated all over the place when the frills were removed. But however difficult and unpopular, the hard line apparently paid off. According to press reports Billera's austerity "convinced banks that USI can generate cash and is a worthwhile credit risk."

In another sad free-spending saga a Midwestern machinery company was wrung dry by the ravages of push-pull inflation. Acting in desperation a worries-plagued board dumped the president and brought in a manager to trim the frills and restore the operation to solvency. His approach was as basic as introducing fresh air as a remedy for suffocation. The first mandate was to cost-justify all dollars spent—on people, projects, things.

Programs with too much "maybe" built into them were eliminated. The new chief checked operating departments to learn who was doing the work and who was getting the free ride. Here, an assistant was fired and his boss put back to work; there, a boss was fired and his assistant promoted.

Scores of association memberships were examined, and

so were subscriptions to magazines and newsletter services. None were arbitrarily canceled, but managers were required to submit periodic reports spelling out the benefits derived. The result was dozens of voluntary dropouts. An insider notes, "Some of these people have magazines stacked two feet high that are still in their wrappings. Others belong to trade associations but haven't attended a meeting in years."

Within four months the company showed its first profit in over two years. Today, it is free of frills and flourishing.

Goldplating has about the same impact on management objectives as thumbing your nose at a customer. A small technically oriented firm near Atlanta produces highly specialized industrial controls. Its engineering staff is made up of top-rated, creative, dedicated professionals. But a young marketing hotshot who two years ago put a hundred thousand inherited dollars into the operation runs the show as if he's in show business. His office looks like a Persian brothel. The chief financial executive's office—for some reason there's more than one financial officer—is similarly decked out. A conference room done up in velvets and teakwood sits idle most of the time. A sophisticated communications system includes closed circuit TV. A computer, used about two hours daily, is also on hand.

The product line is impressive. Even more impressive are items still on the drawing boards. But the business is strapped for funds; its most pressing need is financing. The marketing man, a glib spellbinder type, recently interested a large, well-heeled company in the operation enough to induce its principals to fly in to look over the plant and the books. When the visiting delegation of top brass and accountants arrived, the first move was to take them on a tour of the facilities. That's as far as they got. After taking one look at the apparent excesses, they didn't look further.

The trouble is people get carried away. In a status-symbol society it's easy to make goldplating a way of life on the job. Fancy offices, plush reception rooms, and clever gadgets become synonymous with success and importance. If XYZ, Inc., orders a computer, ABC, Inc., wants one too, sometimes whether it needs one or not. Keeping up with competitors has become as much of a national pastime as keeping up with the Joneses in suburbia. With Jonesmanship in mind, one of the most familiar lumps-in-the-bull pastures of Blunderland is the fertilizer served up by purveyors of plant and office efficiency systems featuring computer hardware and software. I recently had a conversation with an engineering project supervisor in a mammoth New Jersey Army communications center. In describing his work he made occasional reference to "my computer."

"What do you mean by 'my computer'?" I asked.

"Don't tell me you have your own private machine?"

"No, it's used by my group of six people."

Further probing revealed he didn't really need a computer at all. It was more a nuisance than an aid. He got less than 10 percent utilization out of it and prized his slide rule more highly. "If I get truly significant information from the system once or twice a month, it's a lot," he confided. "But if I didn't have access to it, my status would sink. It would actually hurt my career."

Lest there be any misunderstanding, I will readily concede that the computer may be the most important management tool since horse trading began. But however impressive its capabilities, unless the unit can be cost-justified, it's nothing more than a frill.

I cannot ever recall having met the head of a large or small organization whose ego wasn't as big as his job. But the most successful businessmen I know are the ones who have learned to channel their egos constructively. These men and women have enough savvy to realize that excess vanity far too often produces organizational indigestion. When that happens the surgeon usually summoned is the manager with enough know-how to differentiate between the valid tools and the frills, plus the competence to pare down the operation effectively.

Particularly if you run a small, specialized business, the evidence repeatedly testifies that the best way to beat out the competition is by running a fat-free operation. A data-processing firm outside of Baltimore is set up in an old warehouse it purchased outright for a pittance. Its main function is to run payrolls and billing for companies too small to afford their own data-processing setup. The owner-president, who employs eleven clerks and technicians, notes, "We have all the space we need and space for expansion as well." An experienced systems manager, he has procedures down to a science. He sets up a single program to run four or five payrolls at once, and does the same thing with billing. The result is maximum efficiency and productivity. Nor is it a cheapo operation. Top technical people are well paid and well motivated by profit-sharing incentives.

Customers visit the shop on occasion. One remarked recently, "How can you operate in a dump like this?" The chief smiled. "It's easy. By keeping costs down I ensure your business. Or would you rather work with—" he named a key competitor "—who operates out of fancy facilities, has triple my overhead, and charges premium rates to support it?" The customer got the message at once.

Mike Dorota, a gifted Ukrainian-born businessman, pyramided a meager investment into a $1-million enterprise on this philosophy and approach. His company, Apex Electronics, Inc., in Passaic, New Jersey, makes the guns for television tubes, as well as electronics components. Its quality and reputation are second to none. Situated in an old, low-cost neighborhood, Dorota's overhead is a fraction of his competitors.

During the past few years, hit hard by inflation-recession, high costs drove half of the competition into bankruptcy. But his operation continues to flourish. At bankruptcy and distress sales he buys equipment and parts that would cost him ten times as much in the marketplace. His top-level technologists rebuild and redesign equipment until it runs better than new. Because he treats people well, he earns the kind of loyalty that's uncommon today. His office is furnished in 1936 early American—a second-hand desk here, an old cabinet there. There's no carpeting in sight. He does without a reception room. Competitors laugh at his thrift. Effervescent Dorota laughs with them—all the way to the bank.

The trick in attempting to trim or avoid frills lies in knowing where to draw the line, namely in using careful judgment to determine where sound economy leaves off and cheapo tactics take over. Where the judgment is misapplied, the ultimate cost can add up to more than the saving. Take the Eastern Air Lines experience. Prior to 1963, when Floyd Hall moved into the pilot's seat, Eastern had hacked away so hard at frills it dented passenger service. Reports *Business Week*, "We hate Eastern Air Lines" clubs abounded throughout the system. Its slogan, "The great silver fleet," was derided as "The great stingy fleet."

Clearly the idea is to trim frills without trimming the customer, a practice that inevitably backfires.

CHAPTER 9

Programmed Dehumanization

All hail the automated age of the programmer. Computers are programmed. Machine tools are programmed. Entire factories are programmed. Even some people are programmed. What's the consequence of these multiplicitous programs? To give progress its due, it often adds up to faster, more efficient, more reliable output.

The problem lies with the push-and-pull manager, who mindlessly pulls his people apart while pushing out surveys, analyses, and reports. The danger in a superprogrammed society lies in the deadly social and organizational trap of Programmed Dehumanization.

Programmed Dehumanization insinuates itself into our system and mores in a variety of ways. As a by-product of automated productivity improvement, managers are sometimes developed into transaction handlers instead of people handlers. Visit any large paper-processing center, and what do you see? Objectives set in terms of transactions handled: words typed per hour, cards keypunched per hour, invoices processed per hour. When individuals or work groups are evaluated, it's in terms of hourly output.

Conceptually there's nothing wrong with a system

designed to shuffle papers expeditiously. When machine logic supplants common sense, however, human sensitivities get battered and bruised.

In a Connecticut insurance company the vacation schedule was plotted largely by the computer. A periodic print-out predicting workload expectation for the days ahead determined the size of the work force that would be required on a week-by-week, month-by-month basis. One June day Marie, a long-standing, loyal, and reliable statistician, asked her department head if one of the two vacation weeks she was entitled to could be the last week of July. Her sister, she explained, would be visiting her at that time. The busy manager, concealing his annoyance at the request, which should have gone through channels in the accustomed routine, consulted his latest IBM run-off.

"I'm sorry," he replied, "that's one of our peak summer weeks. A full staff will be needed."

"But," the employee protested, "my sister . . ."

"I'm sorry." Her boss cut her off brusquely. "There's not a thing I can do about it. We have to go by the print-outs."

He went by the print-outs; Marie simply went. She handed in her resignation a few weeks later after finding another job that was scheduled to start after her sister's departure. Marie hadn't seen her sister and family who lived in California for almost six years. The last week in July was the only time her sister could visit, and nothing in the world —not even a computer—was going to stop her from taking the week off. Her boss was not only deprived of her presence during that crucial week but had to go to the time and expense of hiring and training a new employee to take over an important and complicated job.

When managerial behavior gets programmed along with electronic equipment, the result is often disruptive. Recently I came across a large toy company's *Executive Policy Manual,* which contained the following pronouncement:

The productive output of all employees is to be monitored and measured on an ongoing basis. Where, for any reason, productivity falls below the acceptable job standard, corrective action must be taken at once.

Evidence indicates that an unproductive employee is an unhappy employee. If corrective action cannot be taken the nonproducer must be dismissed for the good of the company and in his own best interests.

Failure to take corrective action in such cases or to initiate discharge proceedings as required shall be construed as a sign of managerial weakness and irresponsibility.

Again, conceptually, an argument can be made for this doctrine. Organizational deadwood produces organizational rot. But it's not all that clear-cut or precise. A balance must be maintained. We're talking about people, not cedar or ash. If organizational policy is to be effective, it must regard employees as individuals, not faceless automatons. The trouble with programmed rulebook management is that it too often gets wagged by the program.

A case in point is a sixty-one-year-old accounting department employee who was fired one Friday afternoon after twenty-six years of continuous employment. He was told by his boss that a departmental reorganization had made his job obsolete. He was handed a month's severance pay and informed he needn't bother to show up on Monday.

Unpleasant or not, according to the *Executive Policy Manual,* it was a job that had to be done. The employee's thirty-two-year-old supervisor, his reasoning programmed by the system, had no intention of being judged "irresponsible" or "weak" by his superiors. He followed to the letter the prescribed procedure as outlined in Part IV, Section C, Page 28, of the *Manual* for the "Handling of the Nonproductive Employee."

The poor guy on the chopping block understood the operation, and had proven his loyalty and competence over the years. Ten more months would have qualified him for early retirement. Any number of reasonably productive jobs could have been found for him in the interim.

Instead he was sacked by a bottom-line buster, with magnetic bits where his head and heart should have been. When informed of the news, the unfortunate victim was stunned. Had he been a coronary candidate, the firing might well have turned the trick.

He kept repeating to friends and associates, "Twenty-six years of my life, and what have I got to show for it? A month's severance pay."

Coworkers, friends, neighbors, and casual acquaintances were outraged and shocked. Disregarding the stark immorality of the dismissal, consider the consequences of the bitterness, fear, and plunge in morale of the remaining employees on the heels of the action.

Inevitably, the word "programmed" conjures up visions of churning computers and spinning reels of tape. The electronic brain has been touted by maker and user alike as the biggest boon to mankind since the invention of the wheel. Maybe it is. Thanks to the computer we are able to grind out more transactions, more documents, and aid decision making more efficiently than ever before. And who can argue with efficiency?

But too much machine-bred efficiency can produce a breakdown of the system. We've seen it happen, and when it does, the monster starts to devour itself. Marshall McLuhan talks about GM's Lordstown operation as a classic example, although others dispute his contention. Billed as the world's most automated plant, he points out, efficiency was refined there to the dimensions of a flea's hind leg. It was a programmed miracle, a paragon of technoscientific management. Only one thing went wrong. The operation collapsed because people wouldn't work there.

Technology, notes McLuhan, was raised to a peak of obsolescence. Speedup brought slowdown. The decision makers, systems wizards, programmers, and planners were so busy developing a mechanized Mecca where productivity was Allah that no one ever thought to ask, "How do you program job satisfaction into the setup?"

Programmed Dehumanization undermines organizational objectives while it thwarts individual goals, whether it stems from mindless enslavement to a system, rulebook, or electronic machine. The wise and sensitive manager remains wary of this perilous pitfall and takes steps to avoid it.

Some years back a couple of managers from one of the nation's giant aerospace equipment corporations resigned to form a little firm of their own. In a tight and well-knit operation employing fifty to seventy-five people, teamwork and camaraderie thrived; employees were proud of the high-quality products they produced, and the enterprise prospered. As the company continued to grow, increasing numbers of people were hired, until in time loss of simple communications and the personal touch put a damper on the small-company spirit that had previously existed. Despite reasonably high compensation workers no longer felt the personal identification with management, supervision, and each other that used to be present.

To restore the old esprit the plant was rearranged into twelve "profit center" units—in effect, a dozen small companies. "Now," says a spokesman, "people no longer feel like extensions of the assembly line." Productivity has boomed since the change.

The more we encounter this reasoned approach and philosophy in the future, the more effective and productive organizations and individuals will become and the more "performance" we'll see. Clearly there is only one practical solution to Programmed Dehumanization, whatever the form that it takes. That's Rational Rehumanization, sensitively and wisely applied.

CHAPTER 10

Marketplace Myopia

Learn who your customers are. Find out what they want, and respond to their needs. How often this simple and basic counsel is disregarded. Evidence shows that a long list of U.S. organizations, giant sophisticates among them, suffer in varying degrees from Marketplace Myopia. They fail to take a reading of the marketplace; they don't home in on what customers or clients really want and need. The shock effects from such negligence can jolt the foundations of a corporation, institution, or agency, and lead to shattering shake-ups.

The casualty list is sobering. A few years back two chemical giants lost a fortune when they attempted to sell "permanent" antifreeze to customers already content with a lower-priced high-quality permanent product. A major oil company's failure to take the market pulse accurately when it introduced an overpriced high-octane gasoline product cost the company an estimated $20 million. A food-producing behemoth went for a bundle when it marketed a new gourmet line without adequate testing or know-how about customer demand.

A home appliance dealer, a short bus ride from Chicago, invested big money in European plants that manufactured space heaters. The units were fine, high quality, well performing. What went wrong was the marketplace sniffing. The dealer failed to anticipate that central heating would gain acceptance on the Continent and that the whole product line would tend to become obsolete.

The rewards of shrewd and reasoned pulse taking can be every bit as high as the penalties of failure. This holds true if you're a giant Pittsburgh manufacturer or a pygmy in Knoxville, Iowa, where retailer D. J. Witherspoon started a jazzy discount operation called Pamida, Inc. The first Pamida enterprise was a broken-down storefront hastily made presentable by a patchwork carpentry job.

But with the right mix of marketplace savvy thrown in, the venture was destined for success from the start. On opening day milling crowds of customers had to be let in a group at a time. Witherspoon had been cagey enough to assess the pulse of the people and the times. Shoppers in rural areas were starved for bargains, he had reasoned—items obtainable only by making a long trip to the city. What was Pamida's reward? The small investment has been parlayed into a prosperous chain of almost 200 outlets.

Many companies go to a great deal of trouble to gauge the marketplace mood before mass producing a new product. But once the item begins yielding revenue, the tendency often runs toward complacency—another faux pas of substantial proportions. The trick is to engage in pulse taking continuously on a variety of levels and to watch the ever-shifting winds without letup.

Customers do not always know what they want or what's best for them in this climate of me-too, band-hopping management. When the market does know what it needs, the product doesn't necessarily coincide with what salesmen would most like to peddle. As a breed salesmen tend to push the items they can sell with least effort. It is not in their nature to investigate and probe. Except in rare cases they are creatures of habit and custom.

A couple of years back a savvy sales supervisor was put in charge of a New York-based lingerie company's Midwestern region. An experienced pro, he wondered why, since staples sold well, new products and specialty items moved hardly at all. He trained salesmen to explore the potential of these products by specific market groups and locations. Within five months volume shot up more than 40 percent.

The challenge is to pinpoint with reasonable accuracy what people really want and need. Delve deeply enough into this, and you could make a life study of it, as indeed some people do. Some of the computerized programs aimed at gauging market acceptance would have made Einstein blink. And for some marketers the strategy makes sense. No quarrel is made with sophisticated technology if it is rationally applied.

The mismanagement pitfall under scrutiny here is losing sight of the most effective marketing strategy of all: finding out what the customer wants simply by asking him. A few years ago a government-funded agency was set up in a Pennsylvania community to help the disadvantaged poor seek welfare alternatives via "bootstrap" self-help and training programs. The venture started modestly enough, manned by a tight staff of dedicated social workers. They were good listeners, and they responded to human needs as they viewed them firsthand. In those early days its achievements were impressive.

But as the welfare rolls swelled and the client population mushroomed, the agency expanded in size and personnel. Its perspectives grew fuzzy and distorted. It lost touch with the people, and its effectiveness started to wane. Today, the organization is still in existence—very much so. Bigger than ever in funding and scope, its chief god is bureaucracy. It caters more to politicians than to the people it is supposed to be serving. Now primarily a handout distribution center, its contribution to self-improvement and the upgrading of human dignity would be hard to define.

Another by-product trap whereby organizations can lose touch with their markets is the generation of extras and frills that don't pay their way. I have heard these referred to as "lollipops"—expensive, pretty cellophane wrapping, with little if any real value.

Too many "lollipops" can send an operation slithering right up the wall. A California computer maker, in fact, was sent so far up that it almost went over. In a superambitious bid to broaden its sales base it announced with much fanfare that exciting new hardware was available to customers wishing to streamline their management information systems. Virtually from the day the hardware was introduced, it was apparent it was creating little if any excitement among customers. Even if red, white, and blue flares had been attached that exploded into color to the accompaniment of "Dixie" when the "on" button was pressed, it would have produced little more than yawns. The new product flopped with a sickening thud.

The computer was conceptually sound, but it contained so many doodads and attachments that it confused customers and priced itself out of the market in the process. As one industry expert defined it, the trouble was that the producer lacked understanding of his market at the time. New companies were working hectically to offer simpler systems at lower cost. Wary computer buyers, once burned by overpriced, overtouted hardware, were steadfastly determined it wouldn't happen again. The manufacturer should have been aware of this.

To avoid similar blunders a new breed of market-oriented managers places high priority on touching base with their outlets. Olin Mathieson, for one, regularly checks with customers to get their reaction to services and keep real needs in perspective. SKF Industries, Inc., sends production people, engineers, and other internalists to customer plants. Employees see products they worked on and helped to design used in the manufacture of helicopters, rail cars, and other equipment. Customers air their wishes and gripes and suggest improvements. Relationships are personalized and the importance of quality hammered home, where it will do the most good.

Ex-Cell-O Corp. has a similar program. Plant personnel accompany salesmen on calls. When customer complaints filter in, they're posted on bulletin boards for all to see. Department heads meet regularly to identify customer needs and see that they're met. And the company lets its people know what it tells customers through its ads and in person. The value of such communication would be hard to overstate.

The failure to coordinate marketing promises and claims with employee actions and statements creates untold customer ill will and loss of confidence and orders. Recently a New Jersey industrial cooling equipment salesman called on a prospect in the glassware manufacturing line who had expressed interest in his company's products. During the course of the interview the prospect wanted to know what function was served by the product's repositioned support arms.

The salesman went blank. "Repositioned support arms?"

The prospect showed him a trade magazine ad where the feature was described. A recent innovation, it was news to the salesman. The prospect, needless to say, was less than impressed.

Who was at fault—the salesman, his company, or both?

Whatever the answer, one thing is certain: stay responsive to the customers you serve—to their needs, wants, problems, questions, apprehensions, and fears—and you will get the business you need to survive. If you believe you can make your customers swallow what you want them to swallow, your competitors will take over the market.

CHAPTER 11

Bullshevism

Few characters are more interesting and provocative than the Bullsheviks of free enterprise, unless you happen to be one of their victims.

The applesauce merchants of the public and private sectors, entertaining or not, can lay claim to innumerable organizations and marks deftly sent to the cleaners. Consider, for example, the well-publicized saga of Equity Funding Corp. of America.

The forty-six-year old markitect of Equity Funding was Stanley Goldblum, a king Bullshevik of our times. A financial genius of sorts, he traded on the investor psychology of the mad money days of the sixties. He knew you can make people believe what they want to believe. When the quick-buck bait is dangled, imaginations can be stretched to unimagined lengths.

Goldblum was a stretcher sublime. Mod dresser, frequenter of ultralush resorts, red Rolls Royce driver, his operation was described by one analyst as "a blue suede shoes, hipster-type outfit." His style should have given him away, but it didn't.

The fast-talking ex-butcher built a life insurance behemoth. Touted by Wall Street dupes as a "hot property," institutional investors stood in line to buy the stock, while the price climbed higher than ragweed.

In an elaborate and fanciful reinsurance scheme Equity Funding made nonexistent policyholders materialize out of hot air—50,000 of them, according to California's Insurance Department—then sold them to insurance companies. In the inadequately monitored insurance industry no one looked closely enough to uncover the fraud.

Supposedly sophisticated bankers, analysts, and institutional investors displayed childlike faith in Goldblum, the con man's con man. So sincere and persuasive did he sound in his pitches and presentations that he bilked not only outsiders but scores of his own people as well. On April 5, 1973, when Equity Funding filed under Chapter 10 of the Bankruptcy Act, no less than a hundred banks and other institutions found themselves holding 2 million shares of the company's deluxe-grade wallpaper.

If the easy dollar lure is a favorite fish bait for Blunderland's glib phonies and finaglers, so too are the classic symbols of status and prestige. Blandish the title of "professor" or "doctor" before some people, for example, and credulity shoots up like a rocket. The same thing applies to "general," "senator," "president," and others. Response to such titles is often a blend of hushed reverence and the blind belief that exalted personages of such ilk are incapable of wrongdoing.

People seem to forget that doctors, professors, senators, generals, and presidents are human beings just like the rest of us. If pricked, they bleed. If angered, they blow. If tempted, they may just possibly yield.

Another well-publicized bit of chicanery involved Sure Fail finaglers at Executive Jet Aviation, Inc. (EJA), the once-scandal-ridden air taxi company that was controlled by Penn Central Transportation Co. in its days of deep trouble. Its president at the time was Brigadier General O. F. Lassiter (U.S. Air Force-Retired). Its chairman—he quit in 1968 to become Governor George Wallace's running mate—was former Air Force Chief of Staff Curtis Lemay.

Obviously the outfit was structured on a rock of prestige. One may question the ethics of mortals and managers, but never of generals and kings.

Some minds were changed, of course, by dubious developments at EJA. In the summer of 1970 Lassiter was finally kicked out of the company's Columbus, Ohio, headquarters after nearly embarrassing the operation to extinction, according to press reports.

Lassiter has been characterized as a playboy by some, and worse by others. Whatever the case he was a glib and persuasive charmer. The problem was that his charm was misguided, so much so that the company has been going all out ever since his ejection to live down his image.

As a *Business Week* reporter put it, "Gone is the secret bedroom behind the ladies' restroom that Lassiter maintained, and gone are its shadowy—but bosomy—occupants. Also thousands of nonrevenue flight hours that Lassiter and his associates and friends enjoyed."

Today, he adds, the company is so straightforward in its operation that executives feel obliged to apologize for the lack of glamour. But as one analyst remarks, "Better dull than scandal-ridden or bankrupt."

Not all of the dung that hits the fan these days is motivated by shady or fraudulent objectives. Much of it is unadulterated—and often ill-concealed—propaganda.

Take the work sanctification syndrome, where the pap merchants try to con line employees into believing they would be happier hustling cases or key-punching IBM cards than shopping, watching a ball game, guzzling beer, or doing almost anything else. Maybe you can sell the fun and glory of work to the dynamic decision-making manager, or the guy who plays in a band, or the player who covers left field for the Yankees. But show me an employee who doesn't enjoy a day off more than drudging away at a day-in, day-out job, and I'll show you a looney bin prospect.

It would be stupid to underrate the importance of good attendance to plant and office efficiency or treat lightly the multibillion-dollar bath employee absence imposes on enterprise. But when glib Bullsheviks operate under the premise that they can con battalions of cap screwers, check-mark makers, and typists into believing they will burn in hell or the organization will fold if they take a day off, it's carrying fantasy too far.

Of course, work can be rewarding and fulfilling, especially if you happen to be running the show or if you're one of the privileged minority who hold down unusual and interesting jobs. But for ninety-five out of one hundred employees in government or business the daily routine of posting figures to ledgers, punching millions of holes in thousands of cards, or screwing caps on containers is about as exciting as ironing bedsheets at home—except that the TV is missing. With or without the urging of inspirational pep talks the typical clerical employee, production worker, or shipping or warehouse wage earner shows up at work as an economic necessity. Granted, there are techniques that successfully sweeten the job—incentives and morale-boosting strategies that work. But an abundance of evidence is on hand to confirm that inspirational claptrap regarding the sacred aspects of repetitive tedium isn't one of them.

The extent to which most employees sanctify routine work and the seriousness they assign to packaged pap on the subject are illustrated by an amusing anecdote related by Thomas G. Ayers, president of Commonwealth Edison Co., at the Midwest Conference on Industrial Relations. Tongue-in-cheek or not, the story makes a point.

A corporation president, states Ayers, called his company's employees together for an important meeting. "Ladies and gentlemen," the president said, "for some time now a rumor has been circulating among you. I want to say that the rumor is completely true. On the first of next month our total operation will be converted to automation."

The group became noisy and restless. Raising his hand for silence, the president continued: "I assure you that not a single employee will be laid off. Wages will continue as before. Bonuses will be paid as usual. Holidays, sick pay, and pension benefits will remain unchanged. Every employee will be expected to work one day each week. That day will be Wednesday—Wednesday only."

Complete silence followed. Then, one employee jumped to his feet and said, "What? You mean *every* Wednesday?"

Pap comes wrapped in a variety of packages put together by Bullshevik types, ranging from con men who don't care how they accumulate bucks to glib corporate persuaders out to hoodwink shareholders, employees, and the public. Tanks full of hot air are dispensed by sales reps revved up to boost volume—"and to hell with customer needs." More hot air is hosed out by superficial mismanagers seeking to substitute "personality" and glibness for the hard substance of know-how and work.

How do Bullsheviks fare as a class? Over the long pull they generally lose out; their shovels wind up twisted and bent. Over the short haul I offer a friendly word of advice: be wary, be chary; demand substance, not words.

CHAPTER 12

Turnaround Vision

Take a cue from Durante, "The Schnoz."

The place for a manager's nose is to the wind, not buried deep in his muffler. In tackling problems and considering alternatives the objective isn't so much to shine as a hero today as it is to make decisions that won't backfire tomorrow. What it mainly boils down to is taking the IF Factor properly into consideration, projecting ahead, anticipating consequences of actions proposed, thinking—*and planning*—ahead.

How will the customer respond IF? How will the shareholder respond IF? How will employees respond IF? How will the market respond IF? Let's say you're planning to introduce a new product line. What action will you take IF it flops? What IF it takes off like a jet? What IF customer complaints come flooding in? What IF competitors wage a price war in response? What IF any number of things? Will you be ready to cope with them?

Whatever kind of operation you're in, one thing is certain: ignore the IF Factor, and you're asking for trouble.

Three years ago a nationally known farm equipment producer announced improved tractor models equipped with important plus features. Almost simultaneously a prime competitor seemed to be settling in for a prolonged strike in its plants. The combination of events generated a rush of orders that should have been anticipated but wasn't. It caught the company with its capacity down.

In a hectic scurry of patchwork activity carloads of parts were flown in from distant plants. Having failed to provide adequate stockroom facilities, parts were lined up ceiling high alongside assembly lines. As the torrent of orders poured in, the plant was put on a seven-day round-the-clock operation, costing $2.5 million in premium pay. "Motivating" suppliers to accelerate components delivery cost another $2.5 million. Profits drastically slumped as a consequence.

Second-rate IFmanship can cripple productivity and profits faster than an ice storm in an orange grove. Sometimes, it doesn't take much. In the late sixties, according to *Dun's Review,* lack of foresight in purchasing just one small item caused a major snafu at Union Carbide. The problem started when the printing plant that supplied package labels for a fast-selling consumer item went on strike. This left Carbide with enough labels for just a few days' shipments. The strike lingered on for weeks. Against all company policy no other source of supply for the labels had been set up. "The strike," groans a Carbide executive, "was enough to hold up the entire works."

A major food products supplier hit the market with a summertime dessert item that looked like a sure and pure winner. Consumers ate it up and came back for more. Profit projections were made, followed by broad smiles, handshakes, and hearty pats on the back. Production plans and schedules were set up for the following summer. Winter roared in and thawed out. Summer greened in on schedule, with profit expectations high. They dropped quickly enough. The product was about as popular as a strike vote at a National Association of Manufacturers meeting. The reason: IF-less planners had neglected to calculate the cost of reestablishing the market each year for the highly seasonable product.

One of the costliest failures of turnaround vision is management's failure to gauge the results of accelerating technology. A prime example is the electronic data processing field. Breakthrough electronic data processing systems are announced with great fanfare when they occur, but they're rarely developed overnight. The industry communications media—magazines, newsletters, lectures, seminars, and trade association programs—maintain a running dialogue on advances on the boards and in the offing. The alert and informed manager with electronic data processing responsibility stays up-to-date about what is happening and what to expect. His ostrichlike counterpart gets burned.

The administrators of a 600-bed New England hospital ordered a popular model computer a few years back. Innumerable man-hours were invested in it, as well as a lot of money to program it and get the system designed. Two months before scheduled delivery and installation the order was canceled and a new model ordered. The reason was that a management-consulting firm hired by the hospital's controller had conducted a feasibility study and produced hard figures to prove that the new model would create patient service benefits and cost reductions the canceled model could not possibly match.

As a result the design and programming investment was written off and added to the cost of developing a revamped system that was critically needed. Had the institution's financial and data processing executives kept up-to-date on developments, as they should have done, they would have realized several months earlier that the computer on order would soon be outmoded by the new and more efficient model and made their plans in plenty of time to save thousands of dollars.

Over a ten-year period a large manufacturer of tape and recording equipment brought twenty major products to market at a staggering research and development cost. Seven of these items were made obsolete after short-lived stints in the marketplace by the company's own technological advances. At least one other product never even reached the market despite millions of dollars pumped into tooling, research and development, and inventory. The project was written off because new techniques made it obsolete. More than product ventures get stymied by misguided planning and hindsighted management. Here-and-now bucksmanship, as one printing plant could attest, can roast an operation faster than nuts on a griddle. The company ran a large, ancient press, which not only groaned like a ten-ton truck run without oil but also broke down consistently. The unit, which would have cost a pile to replace, was in frequent repair, using spit-and-gum tactics. The machine should have been junked years ago.

In such a profitable enterprise financing a new press would have been no major problem. The chief kept deferring the action. The big capital investment, he reasoned, would reflect poorly on current earnings statements and hack a hole in the period's profits. Unfortunately this manager's long-range perspective didn't match his limited vision. Nor could he picture the consequences of his myopic approach. Press failures produced work failures, causing customers to question the operation's reliability. Important jobs were delayed, causing customer tempers to flare. When customers visited the plant and observed the worn-out, dying relic, they left wondering about the company's solvency. One day as was inevitable the press thonked to a final, agonized, this-is-it halt. Its demise came at an inopportune time when the plant was flooded with orders. It left capacity woefully crippled. Customers began to desert. So in time did the chief, at the Board of Directors' request.

Turnaround vision can be even more devastating when it applies to people instead of products or facilities. In a large federal agency, one of the octopal sproutings of the Department of Health, Education and Welfare (HEW), a behavioral specialist was brought in to determine why the only thing lower than morale was productivity. The conclusion he reached centered on poor people management, in general, and promotion policy, in particular. When key job opportunities opened up, they were almost consistently filled from outside because management lacked the foresight to train and develop employees for advancement.

In the early seventies a nationally known building products company's profits suddenly began to decline. When management consultants were retained in an effort to get at the cause, what they found was revealing. The organization was fairly loaded with talent. But the president and other high-level executives had failed to provide for succession. The result was deteriorating morale at key management levels. Interviews had been conducted in confidence, with anonymity assured. But the consultant said this much, "I've never seen so much shopping around in all my experience." It's no wonder that no one gave much of a damn about the company, or its objectives and aims.

The outcome of virtually all plans we make is conditional. The best problem-solving strategy you come up with, however well intentioned and ingeniously conceived, will backfire IF you don't win the approval and support of key parties concerned. One week during the late sixties an explosive situation developed on an Ohio college campus. Due largely to the intransigence of certain faculty members who were throwbacks to the forties, student revolt seemed close at hand. Already bricks had been hurled through administrative windows. Rumors of a boycott and sit-in were rife.

The president, a would-be progressive, tried to view both sides of the controversy. He decided to take matters into his own hands and worked out a plan for student representation at trustee and administrative conclaves. Fully expecting an enthusiastic student response and a cooling of tempers, he announced his decision on campus. It had little if any effect. The reason was simple. His decision had been reached unilaterally, without consulting the students. As an outside expert later observed, "Had they been given a voice in the matter, my guess is that the plan would have worked like a dream."

In a corporate situation, a producer of small aircraft was threatened with a takeover by a large leisure products company. The prospect gave principals the shudders. In their eyes acquisition by that predator would be a fate worse than bankruptcy. The decision was a fight to the death if need be. The strategy, carefully formulated, was to make certain acquisitions of their own to dilute the holdings of the raider. Two companies were selected, both amicable in response to overtures. The wheels were set into motion. Everything looked rosy. The plan seemed sure to work.

It didn't even come close because management had neglected to get stockholder consent to the proposed acquisitions. In the end the company was barred from making the moves by a stock exchange ruling. In order to win back its listing, the acquisitions had to be rescinded.

When turnaround vision blurs shabby performance, it stacks the deck against profits. No matter how often you shuffle the cards, they will be premarked to beat you. What better example than the losing hand dealt to Boeing in the fog-filled days of the sixties. Certainly the business press has kept this no secret. As 1965 drew to a close Boeing had orders for 418 airplanes, worth more than $2 billion. By the end of 1966 the backlog figure declined to 367. It fell further to 328 by year-end 1967, and it continued to drop steadily. By the time Christmas of 1969 rolled around, only 132 planes, with a value of $1.118 billion, were on order.

Even in the face of this steady decline, notes one editor, "Concern was not deep nor widespread." Actually it wasn't until mid-1970 that a dazed chief eagle and his wonder-birds came to life and faced the realization that unless something drastic was done in a hurry, the operation was headed for Flopsville. When the sleeping monster eventually awoke, massive firings took place, followed by a crash turnaround effort during which planners started to plan. Had sound planning been initiated three or four years earlier, the situation might have been far less traumatic.

What is to be learned from this and other experiences? Confucius put it all in a nutshell, "If a man takes no thought about what is distant, he will find sorrow near at hand." He must have had the IF Factor in mind.

CHAPTER 13

Status Quo Rigidity

Francis Bacon said it over three centuries ago, "He that will not apply new remedies must expect new evils." The evils that are likely to plague the inflexible statisticians of Blunderland would be too numerous to cite.

The president of a medium-size company that has been making a line of packaged food products for more than sixty years is fond of boasting, "We use the same ingredients, equipment and processes today that we did thirty years ago. The same high quality goes into our products."

"The guy's got his head in the clouds," observes one of his primary competitors. "The high quality he's crowing about isn't high enough for today's marketplace. Improved processes have been developed over the past few decades, new machinery and ingredients introduced. The company is twenty years behind the times. Its items are less tasty and more expensive to produce than those of competitors."

The corporation's declining fortunes and diminishing customer roster would appear to back up this contention.

Another case in point is illustrated by the contrast between the operating philosophy of profit-based companies and nationalized enterprises. In the profit-geared operation, where management must account to shareholders and directors for their decisions and results, a reasonable degree of flexibility and dynamism is required for competitive survival if for no other reason. The profit-motivated enterprise that is totally unresponsive to the pressures of change will soon be forced out of the marketplace. In the nationalized organization, where status quo rigidity encompasses adherence to bureaucratic practices that multiply costs and pyramid inefficiency, the sick performance puts nobody's job on the line. The socio-bureaucracy rarely goes out of business. It simply grows increasingly nonproductive and unwieldy, a growing strain on the economy in general and the taxpayer in particular.

A classic example is found in poor pound-beaten England where, according to *Fortune,* the National Coal Board ranked last among five competitors, British Airways last among seven, British Railways last among eight, British Steel last among ten, and the Electricity Council ninth among the ten utilities surveyed. To point up the pitfalls of status quo bureaucratization, British Steel, which has less sales than August ThyssenHütte, employs 230,000 workers. Its German competitor has only 92,000 on the payroll.

Status quo rigidity shows up in other ways as well. Last year a bright young Yale graduate, a marketing major, after on-campus interviews with several corporate recruiters, opted for employment as a manufacturer's rep trainee with an electronics producer. Ranking among the top 10 percent of his class, he was understandably selective.

"What impressed me most," he confessed, "was the company's manpower development program."

This involved, as he viewed it, a series of sophisticated audiovisual presentations as part of an exciting in-house program, which included "comprehensive shirtsleeve work sessions," where managers, supervisors, veteran sales reps, and sales trainees batted problems about. All of this was to center around, and be supplemented by, six months of intensive field experience. The main focus was on action.

The young man was fired up when he reported to

work, prepared to conquer the business world and advance rapidly through the ranks. What he encountered instead was instant disenchantment. The development package as touted by the recruiter and the recruitment literature bore only a superficial resemblance to the training realities.

The in-house portion was tinseled with high-sounding labels and strategies. Lip service was paid to such management concepts as "job enrichment," "multimedia indoctrination," and "managerial grid." But what it actually boiled down to was uninspiring classroom instruction by uninspired instructors.

"After four years of school," said the recruit, "that's all that I needed!"

The field experience was even worse. Trainees in this company were turned over to veteran salesmen, "guidance counselor" types. Conceptually the idea had merit. But the seniors were inadequately motivated. They lacked a sufficient stake in the recruit's success in terms of personal recognition and compensation.

Most older salesmen are already settled into comfortable ruts, a satisfactory income, and good fringe benefits. They possess neither the inclination nor impetus to increase their job time commitment and workload. They're contented with the status quo. Superficially, of course, they are all gung ho for the new recruits. But beneath the facade an underlying resentment is felt for what one senior rep refers to as the new breed of "brash young hotshots." And a layer beneath that abides the job security threat posed by ambitious world-beaters, willing to work and think hard for advancement.

In essence this company's field training has degenerated into the archaic apprenticeship system, where the trainee accompanies the veteran on his rounds, performing small chores and minor functions.

"Half the time," fumes the Yale man, "I was ordered about; the other half I was lectured on tired principles of salesmanship or forced to listen to the old guy's inflated opinions of himself and his virtues. It was a humiliating experience. I finally decided that I didn't bust a gut for four years in school to wind up as a bag-carrying flunky."

He resigned in three months and took what knowledge and experience he had acquired to a competitor. Here the in-house program called for six weeks of preliminary briefing, with the stress mainly on action, involvement, and personal participation. Field problems were set up and re-enacted, interviews and presentations role-played. Motivations were carefully established all down the line, so that trainee success and senior rep success were inextricably linked. The caste system had been all but eliminated. To the maximum degree possible trainees were treated as equals.

After six weeks a trainee was turned out into the field. He covered lesser prospects and customers for a starter. He was handed increased responsibility as his work showed that it merited it. As his need for independence and his ability to fly solo were demonstrated, joint senior-trainee coverage was gradually diminished.

This company's sales manager states: "Today's bright young people are unwilling to sit still for deadening, long-term apprenticeships which sap their spirit and ambition. They want to be thrown into the breach just as soon as they can."

Is there risk involved? Of course, but it's significant to note that in the first company cited, turnover among recruits is double the industry rate. In the second company it's less than half. The first company's market share has been slowly declining in recent years. The second's is gradually building. The lesson is apparent. Where status quo rigidity is abandoned, the profit payoff is inevitable.

One's individual problem may be personal, business, or social. Whatever it is, the solution is probably change, initiating something that is different and new, be it a product, system, training program, or philosophy of handling people. Because mankind through the ages possessed the ambition, intelligence, and balls to conquer imperfection with change,

it overcame difficulties and made headway. In this respect
the commercial enterprise, public institution, or government
agency has much in common with the individual; it solves
problems by responding with change. Since the recorded be-
ginnings of time, whether the organization involved was one's
community, workplace, or home, the responder moved for-
ward and grew; the statustician remained static and, thus
immobilized, became numb.

CHAPTER 14

Cranial Sabotage

The bird is considered by some to be the world's fastest-moving creature. According to *The World Book Encyclopedia*, the speed of the powerful peregrine falcon is estimated at 180 miles per hour when it swoops on its prey.

The idea man shapes up at times like the world's slowest-moving creature, slower than the 0.03 miles per hour of the common garden snail. Under properly adverse conditions he is rendered virtually immobile, a phenomenon one witnesses daily in this nation's offices and plants.

One of the more common causes of cerebracide is the Rip Van Winkle syndrome, better known to decision paralytics as "sleeping on it." A case in point involves a young assistant manager employed by a medium-size city government in a South Central state. A concerned and dedicated professional, he came up with a "technology transfer" proposal for boosting productivity by exchanging information with sister cities nearby, using proven cost-cutting techniques. He spelled out and documented his idea, researching and listing techniques successfully applied elsewhere, along with a practical modus operandi for implementing them at home.

Fired with enthusiasm, convinced that his idea was at least a partial solution to the city's desperate financial problems, he presented it to the city manager. His boss reviewed the proposal, complimented him on his good thinking, and thanked him profusely for his efforts. The young man waited expectantly.

"This shows a great deal of merit," the administrator repeated. "I'd like to sleep on it."

That was two years ago. Despite periodic reminders, he is still fast asleep. By now the young man has all but lost interest.

Projects with noncrucial deadlines are the most apt to get slept on. A nationally known consulting firm counsels clients on how to boost productivity. One area where it has unique and extensive experience is working with hospitals to make health care delivery more efficient. The president decided that a book describing this activity would be a valuable contribution to the management literature and would attract potential clients as well. A well-rated ghost writer was hired to do the book under the president's byline.

Two senior consulting partners are the firm's health care experts. A preliminary meeting was held, with the president, the writer, the two consultants, and the firm's communications director in attendance. A program for the interviewing, research, and writing was set up. The writer got to work on the job.

Phase one was to wade through reams of presentations and reports turned over to him by the communications director. The second phase was to interview several hospital administrators, doctors, and department heads at various institutions who had worked with the consultants. Phase three was the first of three sets of interviews with the consultants. That's where the project began to bog down. It was difficult to touch base with the experts. The interview sessions were scheduled for completion in March; they dragged on till June. After this, according to plan, the writer prepared three chapters and an outline of the book. The communications director was delighted with the result.

The next phase was a review of the material by the president and consultants. Again, the consultants were tied up on "client priorities." Eventually, after repeated delays, it was decided that the material was no longer fresh and timely. The $7,000 fee paid to the writer for work completed to date was written off, and the project abandoned. The writer, a close personal friend, told me that the consultants' noncooperation was deliberate. These fellows were experts on health care; they were the ones who did the dog work. They understandably resented bringing a book to fruition that would be credited to somebody else.

Another Sure Fail way to lobotomize creativity is the popular game of "Who's Boss?" It happened at Genesco while papa Maxey Jarman and son Franklin battled for control of the business. During the skirmishing projects proceeded at a snail's pace, initiative withered, and a long innovacation took place as top aides tried to fathom who would wind up in the driver's seat. A similar situation exists in an Ohio screw products company. Here the twin chiefs are two brothers in conflict. If one says black, the other says white; if one says go, the other says stop. The idea flow in this company has dwindled down to a trickle. A key insider notes, "What one brother turns down the other is apt to approve. It's an exercise in systematic frustration."

At Piper Aircraft Co., when top brass from Bangor Punta Corp. and Chris-Craft Industries were fighting for control of the company, William G. Gunn, the president-at-the-moment, told reporters disconsolately, "Whoever ultimately lands in the top spot is likely to find that serving two masters can be exasperating if not impossible. I just couldn't work, getting two sets of signals."

If "Who's Boss?" leaves a few ideas still breathing, there's another game you might try: "Job Rotation." Conceptually "Job Rotation" makes sense. The idea is to move an individual from one job to another. It makes his job and life more interesting, trains and develops him faster, and provides job coverage insurance when people are on vacation or out sick.

But like any other program if it's mindlessly applied, "Job Rotation" can kill productivity. Training Services, Inc., is a New Jersey firm that sets up training programs and seminars for government and industry. It was recently retained by a city administration to set up a seminar for supervisors and, at the same time, evaluate the unit's training programs.

"One of the first steps," a spokesman recalls, "was a review of programs conducted over the past seven years. What struck us at once was the difference in format and approach from year to year. We saw evidence of good thinking in most of the programs we studied. But each program was dumped the following year and a new program started."

It turned out that the culprit was "Job Rotation." In an effort to upgrade and develop key people, each year a new manager was handed responsibility for the training function. Since training participation and results were highly visible to the unit's chief officer, the new supervisor's first move was to get rid of the existing system and install one of his own, so that he would get credit for it. Enough babies were tossed out with the bath water to comprise a full nursery.

Of course, the old standby guaranteed to build tombstones for brainstorms and embitter innovators in the process is lack of realistic reward. A marketing aide employed by a detergents producer dreamed up a promotion idea that netted thousands of dollars in earnings. The president, with fanfare and flourish, presented him with a personal letter of commendation and thanks. When months passed with no reward more tangible than the letter forthcoming, he showed his opinion of the letter by sending one of his own. It began: "I herewith tender my resignation because . . ."

No person is of more value to an enterprise than the individual with the talent and imagination to dream up good ideas and the courage to promote and pursue them. Applying chintzy treatment to outstanding idea men makes as much sense as feeding third-grade oats to a Kentucky Derby winner. At Diamond Shamrock Corp., according to one press report, a twenty-three-year-old process engineer put his trainee's job on the line by rejecting the advice of senior engineers. Instead, he developed an ingenious way to prevent costly ruptures in an important product—then left the company abruptly when neither promotion nor salary increase followed his contribution. "Under corporate policy," his supervisor sadly explained, "trainees must wait for the normal one-year review."

An interesting aspect of cranial sabotage is that it needn't be directly administered to have its full destructive impact. Some Sure Fail superpros commit cerebracide by proxy, bringing in outsiders to turn off the idea tap.

I was once called in to write a speech for the head of a large manufacturing company (client disguised). I got a rundown on subject matter, audience, and objective from the PR director. He gave me several magazine articles the chief executive admired, plus a manuscript already completed. This was a draft of the speech prepared by one of the company's young PR hopefuls. The PR director gave me the name of the man who had written the speech and told me he was available for information if needed.

I took the material home and reviewed it. The procedure is by no means unusual. Experienced professionals are often called in to do a job because in-house capabilities are weak or because previous attempts have been botched. But this isn't always the case. Here the draft I had been given contained some fine writing and imaginative thinking. It needed polishing in spots but was, all in all, a creditable job.

The next day I called on the young man who had prepared the first draft. He was reluctant to communicate, almost sullen, until I told him I thought he had done an excellent job on the speech. Then he opened up right away. The reason for his initial hostility was clear. He had poured himself into the project, had applied his considerable talent and ability, hoping for the recognition he deserved. Instead, his efforts were slighted; the assignment was turned over to an outsider. His inevitable conclusion was, "Why undergo all the hardship and heartache?"

When I pointed out the speech's merit to the PR director, he agreed that it contained "some good material" and encouraged me to use what I liked. But he insisted I do the final draft. It was easy to see through his reasoning. The chief executive was an unpredictable tyrant. If he was displeased with the speech, the PR man wanted to be on record, on the one hand, as having hired a top-rated pro for the job and, on the other hand, as not having had it come out of his shop. It was his way of covering himself if called on the carpet— and a way to turn off a budding idea man.

The pattern is all too familiar. A consultant is called in to set up a system or supervise a project without considering the feelings of staffers involved. Resentful insiders secretly oppose the innovation—one of the best ways to ensure its demise.

A business school professor once told me, "If I had a dollar for every good money-saving idea shelved by selfish, gutless, or near-sighted managers, I could buy out Exxon, IBM, and General Motors and have enough cash left over to bail New York City out of its difficulties."

He speaks from long, hard experience as a chief executive, consultant, and educator. The number of good ideas shot down each year in organizations public and private, he believes, would probably boggle the imagination. If the truth could be told, some of the reasons and reasoning would line up as follows:

* There's nothing in it for me.
* Too much of a hassle to bring the idea to fruition or too much labor and sweat.
* The timing wasn't right when the suggestion was made.
* I don't like the s.o.b. who came up with the idea.

* It would give an ambitious subordinate too much recognition and credit.
* It would mean sticking my neck out.
* It would mean less power for me and more for somebody else.
* Too radical and drastic a change.
* Too skinflint to shell out the capital investment required.
* Not enough time taken for adequate review and appraisal.
* Executive—or committee—unable, or unwilling, to make decision.

The rhetoric regarding productivity is eloquently echoed at all leveis of management. Executives articulate inspiring aphorisms about its value and need. If the multitude of ideas gestating in employee minds today could be presented and applied, I would venture to guess it would make inflation reel under the impact. All it takes to stimulate good thinking and the expression of thought are the right encouragement, recognition, and credit. I call that creative management. All it takes to turn off the tap are credit hogging, lack of attention, and/or indifference. I call that cremative management.

CHAPTER 15

Scare Tactics

More people flop through fear than from lack of ability. It percolates through one's consciousness, changing the rich wine of creative thought into water.

In a New York City family-owned direct-mail-merchandising company one of "the brothers," the marketing vice president, was a dictatorial tyrant who rode herd on his staff like a tough Army colonel. One afternoon he handed a talented new assistant the task of composing an important piece of promotional copy, his first big assignment.

After a hurried briefing, the vice president growled, "I'm giving you a crack at this, young fellow, because I want to see something fresh and creative around here for a change. I'm fed up to the scalp with this tired old tripe we've been getting."

Although struck with anxiety, the young aide resolved to show his boss what he could do. It was the opportunity for which he had been waiting. Returning to his desk he tackled the project, writing and rewriting. He worked hard for originality and achieved it. His final prose "sung," as they say in the trade. Innovative and sparkling, it was the best piece of writing he had ever turned out.

When he showed it to his boss, the VP's critical eyes

glowered over the pages while the young hopeful stood by nervously, mentally chewing his nails. An occasional grunt could be heard. Then the chief's scowling face darkened. "It's not right," he said. "Too radical. Out of step with our image." Although the copy was fresh and original, what the boss had said he wanted, panic sniped at the aide. No mention had been made of the work's many virtues. It didn't occur to the aide that the boss could be mistaken in his judgment or that the critique might have stemmed from lack of imagination or the sheer perversity of the executive's nature. When the young assistant was given an opportunity to rewrite the material, he was grateful for the reprieve. He had half expected to be sacked on the spot.

The grudgingly approved second draft was safe, trite, and ordinary—much inferior to the first draft. But its acceptance eased the pressures of worry and fear. The young man picked up some misguided savvy from the experience, having learned about the perils of free expression and boat rocking and the dangers of trekking down unexplored paths.

Stories like this are far from uncommon in the stifletoriums of commerce and industry. In an eastern Ohio consumer products company no less than six "design engineers" are regularly commissioned to work up product and container presentations. Typically one package model will be produced internally, another worked up by consulting firm A, a third by consulting firm B, and others by free lancers who work independently for the company.

The vice president who masterminds this extravaganza of duplication is an insecure man. His modus operandi is to pull from each presentation what he believes to be the best features with the maximum sell. Out of this he develops a final model worthy of viewing by the division head. His motivation for "spreading the wealth" is his tyrannical boss's biting sarcasm and a recollection of past heads made to roll because of what the tyrant referred to as "insensate mediocrity."

Running scared, the executive's chief aim is to cover himself. Nor is his rationale in making the multiassignments all that illogical. First, the vice president reasons, he gets the best thinking of his own best people. Second, he puts himself into a position where he can prove to his autocratic boss that maximum effort went into the project. Third, he establishes a "bank" from which to draw replacement ideas when the work he submits is shot down.

The trouble with the arrangement is that what almost inevitably emerges is a potpourri of diverse ideas and artistic styles, an ultimate paste-up job of sorts that is less effective than any one of the individual efforts. Presumably this unwieldy system was contrived by the vice president to temper his superior's displeasure. Remarkably the division chief never thinks to question the methods or exorbitant cost. One recent packaging-design project wound up costing the company almost $200,000. In a more rational, less fear based environment, a superior product would have been created for a third of that price.

Fear can do fearsome things to people. It can trigger rash and unreasoned behavior.

Calvin C. Clements, a top TV writer and idea man, can attest to this from personal experience. Early in his career he was assigned the job of creating a script for a well-known producer. He turned out three drafts in a row. Each time the producer offered vague complaints to explain his rejection. "After the fourth try," Clements recalls, "I decided I had either gone bananas or the guy didn't know what in hell he was talking about. The story lines were sound, the plot work and characterization solid, the themes highly original."

He consulted his agent and others and found out the score. The producer, though earning top money, had a reputation founded on earlier triumphs. His last three shows had been flops. One more failure would throttle him, or so he imagined. So fearful was he of failing again, he kept stalling script approval to delay this possibility.

"The poor guy suffered from decision paralysis," notes

Clements. "His perspectives were shot. He was no longer capable of a sound, reasoned judgment."

Fear of the possible consequences of actions and decisions can ravage an organization. When veteran mismanagers play Caesarian roles and assume medieval sovereign powers, they're apt to scare the bejesus out of their "subjects" at the operation's expense.

A few years ago a Cleveland supermarket manager with outstanding ability found himself boxed into an untenable situation. His store was located in an area where competition was fierce and shoplifting was the "in thing" among teenagers. The manager learned to live with the problem. He developed a sharp team of personnel, set up tight controls, and wrung maximum profits out of the enterprise. Yet with each visit the district's group executive appeared increasingly depressed by the figures. Pressured relentlessly by the chain's top brass, he let fall hints of serious dissatisfaction at headquarters and dangled the hangman's noose as the penalty for continued failure.

Sweating, the distraught manager racked his brain. He put in long hours of overtime, doing everything in his power to inch profits higher. Nothing seemed to work. The potential just wasn't there. When he tried making this clear to his superior, the group executive, fear-driven himself, shook his head dolefully, interpreting the manager's attitude as a sign of weakness. As weeks passed the screws were tightened. In time the manager, in desperation edging on panic, saw himself faced with the alternatives of boosting profits or being summarily dismissed.

He had two children in college. Dismissal would mean loss of crucially needed income and reputation as well. This narrowed the choices to one. He instructed clerks to illicitly mark up merchandise and taught cashiers how to cheat at the registers. He fudged inventory and "shrinkage" records. He showed the increased profit required for survival—until he was caught.

In another tragic situation a new top-management

team stepped into a Massachusetts industrial components manufacturing company. Division sales executives, driven by their chief to milk maximum volume out of field representatives, engaged in scare tactics in an effort to achieve superhuman results. The new president was fond of quoting Harry Truman's famous line about getting out of the kitchen if you can't stand the heat.

Smart salesmen pulled out in droves. But every organization has its hard core of plodders who quake at the prospect of change, lack the confidence to change, or keep *intending* to change but never quite make it.

One fifty-year-old sales pro had been a steady producer for years. Suddenly his boss told him his territory wasn't living up to its potential. The boss kept raising his quota and letting him know that his job would be in jeopardy if he failed to meet it. The salesman worried himself into a state. He rose an hour earlier in the morning and worked an hour later at night. But no sooner was the quota reached than it was hiked again. Convinced that no company would hire a man his age, he tightened his lips and remained.

Inevitably it came to a point where he felt the limit of human effort had been surpassed. He tried to convince his supervisor that every possible nickel was being wrung out of the territory. This was interpreted as "a clear sign of weakness."

A turning point had been reached. The salesman's health already had begun to crumble. Formerly a productive and loyal employee, his new goal was personal survival whatever the cost. He offered kickbacks to selected accounts. It boosted volume but undermined his personal income. Eventually this tragic counterpart of Willie Loman suffered a heart attack and died.

Frightened people rarely function effectively. The author Katherine Mansfield once said, "When I look back on my life all my mistakes have been made because I was afraid." When scare tactics are applied in an effort to achieve unrealistic goals, something must give. Too often it's the individual.

Fear-prodded dishonesty can take more forms than one. In a Midwestern cosmetics company product development was crippled by a chief executive more concerned with penalizing failure than with motivating success. When a new shade of lipstick was produced, for example, it was the custom for several key executives to pass judgment on its market worth and potential. The president himself ultimately approved or rejected the product. But prior to final approval he went through the conference table ritual of scaring the hell out of his aides. The system worked simply enough. One at a time the art director, general manager, purchasing agent, manufacturing VP, and others were put on record regarding their personal comments and preferences.

One manager who is still with the company confided recently, "It's a harrowing experience. The meeting's notes are typed up and held like a guillotine blade over managerial necks."

In the semitangible area of judgment where instinct and taste balance hard data and experience, the chief made a grim and somber rite out of individual projections and views.

After the product's introduction a follow-up ceremony took place. Individual judgments were reviewed, with right guessers publicly complimented on their savvy and wrong guessers scorned as near-incompetents. When products flopped badly, unexplained firings sometimes took place. Inevitably when called upon to make judgments, the overriding concern of managers centered more on self-preservation than on honest evaluation. At conference inquisitions executives hedged on their bets to the maximum degree possible.

One executive, after throwing in the sponge on a $60,000-a-year job, declared:

It became a question of what went first, the money or my self-

respect. It got so that integrity was placed second. I can remember that on one occasion I was so excited over what I
felt to be a new product's potential, I wanted to rave about it.
Instead I found myself murmuring obeisantly that it showed
some promise, but needed more life. The "promise" would
cover me if the product succeeded; the criticism would be on
record if it flopped. I think it was at this point that I decided
to quit.

As a consequence of fear-based evaluation systems of
this type, endless samples and models are needlessly ground
out and paraded on review at an astronomical cost of time,
money, and energy. Product approvals are delayed till the last
minute, and based on critiques voiced insincerely. In the meantime order and production backlogs build. Pressures multiply;
tensions thicken; friction mounts. Yet when one asks this
scaretaker chief what method he endorses to approve and
reject new products, he blithely replies, "Executive consensus,
there's no other way."

Call it consensus, competition, no-nonsense management, whatever you like. Call it by any label you wish, but
if the operation is launched from a springboard of fear, it will
produce creative paralysis, incompetence, goal-defeating
vindictiveness, and worse. As mountains of evidence demon-
strate, when skin preservation comes first, other considerations—including organizational goals—get brushed aside in
the hectic fight for survival.

CHAPTER 16

Social Irresponsibility

It happened last year in Detroit, but it could have happened in Pittsburgh, Boston, New York, or Los Angeles. The time was 3:15 P.M.—broad daylight. A nervous young man, black, aged nineteen, suit draped over one arm, entered a dry-cleaning establishment. He waited quietly while the owner finished serving the store's lone customer, then turned inquiringly toward him.

The black man asked what it would cost to dry clean a suit while a bell tinkled softly as the door closed behir ' the departing customer. The proprietor started to answer but never finished his sentence.

A tense voice said, "Take it easy and do what I say, man. I got a gun under this suit."

The proprietor froze. He could see the barrel peering out at him. In quivering tones the black man directed him to empty the cash register. In the course of this transaction the proprietor reached one hand under the counter—for either an alarm button or a gun the holdup man assumed. Panicking, he pulled the trigger and fled. Seconds later, ordered to halt by a policeman on the sidewalk outside the store, he kept going and was gunned down. An hour later he was dead. The proprietor, who had been shot in the stomach, survived.

A subsequent probe revealed that the black youth had been a loser from the day he was born—he had been in and out of trouble with the police. It also revealed that a year earlier he had been enrolled in a corporate job-training-and-work program for "hard-core unemployables" and had stuck it out eight months, until the program was discontinued by the company as part of a cost-cutting campaign. Surprisingly the holdup man's record had read, "Shows promising potential."

Who was responsible for this young man's wretched, wasted nonlife—the youth himself, brought up in squalor, without dignity, opportunity, or hope; the father who never set eyes on his son; or the mother, bitter, drained, semiliterate, who scrounged for whatever living she could make while her four children more or less shifted for themselves? Or was it a society that preached "equal opportunity" but never quite reached this goal, or a company that briefly flashed a ray of hope and extinguished it when the going got rough, or the government or the business community?

Maybe all of these contributed a little—maybe business even more than a little.

It is no news to anyone that we're a society torn by crises ranging from drugs, crime, and racism to substandard housing, unemployment, and pollution. Should business share in the responsibility for these conditions? You be the judge.

Business is the nation's number one energy consumer, the biggest generator of product and production waste, and thus the nation's foremost polluter. Business, through its state and federal "lobbies" and deals, sets national standards of integrity that in some cases it would be kind to term "shady" or "questionable." Business, because of marginal employment practices in some sectors, helps to shape adversely employee work and performance attitudes and generates rancor and bitterness among minority groups. By virtue of its products, methods of production, and marketing requirements, business spawns congestion, overtaxes transportation, and in some cases creates slums.

Any thoughtful student of business and society will tell you that corporate actions and policies, directly or indirectly, have an impact on the community, influencing standards and life-styles. The single-track managerial ostrich would like to have you think otherwise. Echoing the pronouncements of economist Milton Friedman, he stubbornly proclaims that the only "business of business is business." Of course, the business of business is profits. But when the conduct of business hurts people, over the long pull it's unprofitable to both business and people. The businessman who clings to the outmoded notion that the business of business is business alone has no business being in business.

The pressures for corporate social responsibility are mounting faster today than the shroud of haze over polluted cities. Scores of consumer groups, religious groups, labor groups, environmentalist groups, black groups, ethnic groups, women's groups, senior citizens' groups, and government agencies are monitoring the system with unprecedented fervor.

Angry and resolute, they operate under the not-unreasonable premise that since corporate enterprise contributes its portion of pollution, prejudice, and endangerment to society, it should participate in attempts at social improvement and restructuring—with corporate as well as social survival in mind. What the new militants want ranges from equality, job opportunity, and a safe, clean environment to better health care, crime control, transportation, education, and housing.

Today, we are witnessing dramatically effective organization-planned pressures being applied, which run the gamut from picketing, slowdowns, and strikes to corporate profile smears, annual meeting disruption, "responsible investor" action, student and consumer boycotts, and class action suits.

The evidence keeps proliferating. A New England manufacturing plant was shut down when its odoriferous fumes fouled the area. It's a matter of public record that a citizens' group called Grassroots Action, Inc., incensed by declining telephone service coupled with accelerating rates, mobilized thousands of consumers to press legislators for acceptance of a host of stated demands against The New York Telephone Co. A Midwestern producer of antipersonnel weapons was the prime target of a determined campaign to induce the company "to change its priorities from death to life." The annual meeting of an oil industry giant was made a shambles by demonstrators protesting the company's involvement in apartheid South Africa. A Department of Health in a northern New Jersey town received a spate of citizen complaints when a chemical company's plant discharge discolored a stream.

The blunt reality of the matter is that millions of Americans have had their fill of polluted air and waterways, Pacific oil spills and Washington gut spills, prohibitively expensive health care, deadly dull jobs, and military meddlings in remote hamlets of the world.

People are no longer naive. They are being educated to understand that corporations play a significant role in producing social problems. They are insisting more and more that American business should have a significant role in solving some of these problems. Citizens of the United States desperately want and need—and have every right to expect— socially responsive corporate action, a return to safety and decency. The screws are getting tighter each day. Responsible government officials, social scientists, academicians, futurists, and enlightened businessmen are predicting with social activist David F. Linowes that in the not-too-distant future periodic corporate social audits will be as commonplace in the United States as balance sheets and earnings statements.

Increasingly the message is reaching out over most of America and most of the world. But it eludes the managerial escapist who, ensconced in his fog-misted cubicle, continues intractably to insist that the business of business is business alone and, in the manner of the grub worm, burrows ever more deeply into the bowels of old Mother Earth.

One such all-business businessman, a New England electronics manufacturer, had been polluting local waterways with noxious wastes for years. Starting several months ago increasing pressures were brought to bear by area residents and conservation groups. Having ignored the problem for years, it finally reached the point where the company had to respond. But instead of installing critically needed pollution control equipment, it made a couple of cheap token changes and bribed local officials to approve them in an effort to take off the heat. The ruse worked briefly, and not very well.

The continuing level of pollution caused by the plant was as apparent as ever. One conservation group hired an engineering firm to check out the system. Its report was a shocker; the company was publicly branded an unconscionable polluter. Pressure mounted higher than ever as the corporate profile deteriorated. Its worsening image had a devastating effect on employee morale, already low. Key personnel quit. It became increasingly difficult to recruit good young people.

The board of directors met to decide what action to take. It agreed reluctantly to put in the control system so urgently needed, even though the cost was 30 percent higher than it would have been three years before. Today the company's chief executive unhappily concedes, "Had we done what was right to begin with, it would have saved us considerable heartache and a great deal of money."

A large food-processing plant employing hundreds of Puerto Ricans and blacks has acquired a reputation for its shabby treatment of employees. It operates within legal bounds, but just barely. Despite the social awakening of the seventies and the general rebellion for rights in America the company continues to resist pressures to improve working conditions and provide opportunities for minority workers to advance to supervisory and management jobs.

Token changes have been made in response to the pressures. A small handful of black and Spanish-speaking employees have been upgraded into low-rated supervisory slots. Public pronouncements are issued periodically—via the PR department—affirming the company's deep concern for its people.

But the tokenism is transparent. Morale, always poor, has declined to new lows. Employee resignations are increasing. Pilferage, even sabotage, has become hard to control. Employee grievances are filed at the hint of a conflict. The president, tight-lipped and intractable, takes a warrior's stance. In his view the plant is a battleground, with management and workers in a constant state of siege.

Six months ago the situation reached a point of crisis. A "job action" developed and then a full-blown strike. Non-union personnel worked long hours in an effort to get out the merchandise. It didn't work. Shipments were lost; trucks broke down; billings were garbled. The company was losing thousands of dollars. Negotiations were in progress, but they were supercharged with hostility.

Impatient to spur settlement, the president had another productivity-busting brainstorm. He hired a black Uncle Tom employee-relations manager he knew he could count on to play the role of "company man." Reasoning that "they'll come to terms with one of their own kind more readily than with one of us," he installed this man as a front.

The effect was as dramatic as expected, but it worked in reverse. The new manager lasted exactly ten days, by which time the crew had him pegged to a tee (for Tom). One day the workers' committee stomped out of the bargaining room in a rage. "We'll resume talks," a spokesman told management darkly, "when you fire that fink, not before." The black manager was replaced, and an honest compromise finally reached.

The day is at hand when social responsibility—in its most basic form at least—can no longer be regarded as a management option. In employment and work practices especially, along with such areas as safety and pollution control, it's reaching the point where you either shape up—or else.

The "or else" implies a threat to one's image, which is of overriding importance to most large corporations. But it includes legalistic teeth as well, and these appear to be growing sharper each day. A major oil company shelled out $2 million in back pay to workers whose layoff was deemed discriminatory due to age. A consumer products company was ordered to promote dozens of women to higher-ranking jobs and give them thousands in differential pay because of sex discrimination. Several drug companies are presently bracing themselves for court battles because of alleged product harm to consumers. Eleven integrated oil companies have been sued for allegedly limiting supplies and boosting prices of petroleum products, thus squeezing extra dollars out of U.S. gas and oil users.

Each year, notes *Business Week,* 20 million Americans are injured severely enough in product-related accidents to require medical treatment. Some 110,000 are permanently disabled, and 20,000 die. The cost to the economy is more than $5.5 billion annually. Now, patience has all but run out. Today, those who refuse to comply with the tough new Consumer Product Safety Act are subject to fines ranging from $50,000 to $500,000 and jail terms of up to one year.

As Max Ways points out in *Fortune,* there's a "connection between morality and morale. A managerial group riddled by doubts of its own moral health might lose the internal trust upon which its vigor largely depends."

For decades return on investment has been the ultimate yardstick of corporate performance. But corporate investment involves, and has an effect on, not only financial resources but human resources as well, within the organization and without. However responsible officers and directors may be to shareholders, the owners of the company aren't the only ones who will gain or be hurt by corporate policies, actions, and decisions. Nor are they the only ones who will be in a position to call executives to account and make them answer for socially irresponsible behavior.

CHAPTER 17

The Not-So-Gay Deceivers

Alexander Pope wrote, "Who dares think one thing and another tell, my heart detests him as the gates of hell."

The not-so-gay deceivers of profit and nonprofit enterprise usually bring as much woe on themselves as on others. People who seek to mislead and hoodwink their fellows find it hard to be true to themselves.

Ranked high among the tools of deceit is the insincere promise—the anticipated result or reward recklessly or dishonestly dangled.

Shakespeare referred to promises as "unpaid debts." If this is true, I know some fable-minded managers who are in hock up to their thyroids. To the semiethical businessman a promise is one thing, fulfillment quite another. In fact, some easy-assurance addicts spend half their time making promises and the other half breaking them.

One bitter manager was heard to remark about his ex-boss, "If he stopped making promises, what would he have to forget?"

Hard-to-keep promises, casually given, constitute a perilous pastime, a practice that can backfire with the recoil of a high-powered bazooka or a supercharged cannon if a customer is involved.

An example that comes to mind took place in a Philadelphia printing plant. An equipment supplier had interested the owner in an automatic feed press, a big ticket item. Now with the taste of a fat commission on his tongue, he had brought along his supervisor to help sew up the sale.

The deal sounded attractive to the businessman, especially the trade-in allowance offered on his ancient handpress. When the salesman shoved the contract under his nose, he was ready to sign, but on one condition only.

"It's no deal unless I can have delivery of that press by June fifteenth at the latest. I have a big order coming in. If I miss out on that business, I'll lose a lot of money and probably a customer to boot."

"No sweat," the supervisor assured him. "You'll have it in plenty of time." The customer insisted he write it into the contract.

The deal was made. On June sixth a trucker arrived to pick up the discontinued press. Apprehensive, the partner telephoned the supervisor.

"Are you certain that new machine will get here on time?"

"Don't worry about it. You have my word."

On June twelfth he called again. There would be a slight delay, he was informed. The slight delay extended until the end of July. Unable to handle the large order without the new press, he lost the business. When delivery was finally made, he called the supervisor again.

"I'm accepting the unit because my back's against the wall. But I'm putting you on notice now that I'm suing you for the money I lost because the press wasn't here on time as you promised."

Unlike the supervisor the customer kept his word. He not only sued, but collected.

Another favored ploy used by merchants of deceit is to lie to their people. An example of this occurred recently in the mayor's office of a large Midwestern city. An ambitious

young sociologist was all fired up over an idea he had concocted to help ghetto residents help themselves. With eyes
shining he presented it to his superior, the mayor's top aide.
The proposed program had merit, the manager thought, but
would be too expensive to set up.

If he admitted this to the young enthusiast, however,
it might discourage him, maybe even provoke him to resign.
The idea man was talented and bright. He wanted badly to
keep him on the staff. So he decided to stall him along with
the promise that he would work with him at some later date
to put the program across.

The later date never arrived. In the meantime the
young man was trained and given good field experience. His
value grew steadily, along with the investment of time and
money put into his career. As the months passed he continued
trying to push his idea. When it became clear that his boss
had simply stalled him and had no intention of making good
on his word, he handed in his resignation.

The number of bright young employees who follow
this route each year because of careless promises more care-
lessly broken would be difficult to estimate. If I had to venture
a guess, I'd say it soars well into the thousands.

So many employer-employee relationships begin with
a lie. Is it any wonder a disaster course follows? A sharp young
writer with good management background and training was
interviewed recently by a partner in a nationally known New
York-based consulting firm. The writer knew what he wanted.
He was interested in communications—articles, speeches,
working with the press. In most other industries the job title
would be public relations manager.

The way the firm was set up, such chores were handled
mainly by partners and managers, with help provided as
needed. The partner's chief interest in this man was in his
potential as a composer of client reports and proposals, key
selling tools in consulting.

He discussed this with the candidate. As long as the

major thrust of the job was communications, he replied, he'd be willing to help out with reports from time to time. Consultants are supposed to know better, but the candidate was assured that's the way it would be. As a sign of good faith he was even given the title of communications manager.

The first few weeks of his employment he was given "communications" assignments along with reports. He also received special training and important insights into the business. The partner's brightest hopes were exceeded. The recruit was a report-writing wiz. Within three months time he found himself preparing reports almost exclusively. He complained to his boss, reminding him of their agreement.

"Stick it out a while longer," his boss urged. "You won't be sorry."

He wasn't. In the weeks that followed, the training and experience he received added a priceless dimension to his background. But he was still writing reports.

One morning three months later the partner received a phone call from a competitor with whom he was on a friendly knife-throwing basis.

"Jim [name disguised], I'll never be able to thank you enough."

"For what?" Jim asked suspiciously.

"For the job you did of training Bob Wilson [name disguised]."

"Bob Wilson! Why he's my—"

"I know. I just hired him."

A more subtle but no-less-deceitful and ruinous lie is perpetrated by the top man himself in articles, in speeches, and in person.

The line runs something like this: "However important profits may be, around here they are secondary to people. People come first. Quality is people. Competition is people. Business is people. People constitute the main justification for our existence." El presidente then proceeds to give his people a reaming from which they may never recover.

The promise of a promotion he made to Jones a few months back conveniently slips his mind. He rejects a well-qualified job applicant because he's Jewish, Catholic, Puerto Rican, or black. He exerts undue pressure on Smith to produce beyond his realistic capabilities because Smith is fifty-six years old and afraid to quit or fight back. He steals Delaney's idea and tries to make it look like his own. He encourages a supplier salesman to devote days of work and effort to help him solve a plant problem, then places the order with someone else because he can beat him down 2 percent on the price.

Yet to hear him talk, he goes all-out for people and everyone loves him.

Perhaps the most devastating deception of all is the deception we heap on ourselves. Yet, the sad reality is that some managers plunged into deceivership are more duped by themselves than by others. Classic among this breed is the sequestered high-level executive who is too remote or too busy to find things out for himself. He relies on key aides exclusively as his pipeline to the ranks. In the typically uncontrolled organizational environment the aides serve up information, as follows:

1. By telling the boss only what he wants to hear (how good, how great, how smart he is).
2. By telling him only what they want him to hear (how good, how great, how smart they are).
3. By omitting information that might be embarrassing to tell or personally disadvantageous (about fumblings, misjudgments and low-performance indicators).

The simple truth can solve the most complex of problems. Fiascos like Watergate, major plant strikes, stunning product failures, and organization upheavals more often than not result from a fabric of insincere promises, lies, and distortions—the key components of deceit.

CHAPTER 18

The Cloud 9 Siesta

Success, unmonitored, can become a direct route to failure. Take the case of—we'll call him Bill Jenkins. Two years ago at age thirty-four Bill made something of a name for himself with a large Midwestern manufacturer of electrical products. The company had been undergoing a severe productivity slump and hired Jenkins as personnel manager to remotivate plant and office employees. He had a good industrial relations background and was smart, sensitive, and knew how to get along with people.

Fresh on the job, ambitious, and loaded with energy, Jenkins channeled all of his considerable effort and brainpower into hammering out a motivational program that was exciting and stimulating. He worked closely with line managers and supervisors, devoting long hours of hard thought and study. The program exceeded his, and management's, most hopeful expectations. Absence dropped, rejects fell, morale shot up, and productivity rocketed.

Deservedly Jenkins became an overnight hero. He received wide acclaim for the job he had done. His program was written up in the press, and he was asked to prepare articles for professional journals. The president promoted him to a vice presidential slot. He was nominated as an officer of the local industrial relations society. It was heady fare, and he loved it. With each mark of recognition and acclaim he floated a little bit higher. Finally, reaching Cloud 9, he relaxed and had himself a siesta.

Meanwhile, back in the Real World, things were starting to happen. New conflicts, frictions, and labor problems developed. New standards were set up and challenged. Bill Jenkins was still in charge, but a different Bill Jenkins. Up there on Cloud 9 one gets a rather fuzzy view of Mother Earth. Two years earlier Jenkins would have been right in there in the middle of the fracas working his heart out. Before his rise to glory he maintained close personal contact with the issues and people. He studied and analyzed alternatives, waded courageously into problems, and tackled decisions with vigor. Today, instead of working, he "delegates." He presides from a cumulous tower.

When success goes to the head of a Commander-in-Brief, he becomes so comfortable and complacent sitting on top of the world that he forgets it revolves.

We call the disease "optimiasma"—optimism nourished by wishful dreams. When it is siesta time on Cloud 9, the illusion is created that success breeds success automatically, that sunshine routs storm clouds for good. As the evidence shows, optimiasma is a psychic affliction based on the belief that past performance is enough to buy a free ride for the future. It rarely works that way. As someone once quipped, "The only place success comes before work is in the dictionary."

Nowhere is optimiasma more debilitating than in the case of the managerial climber who reaches a plateau and settles down to enjoy it. A good example is the smart MIT graduate who clawed his way through the ranks of a large Eastern hospital's data processing complex. Advancing rapidly from systems analyst to systems manager, his career was distinguished by a succession of notable achievements. His crowning accomplishment was a brilliant program that streamlined hospital record keeping and added a new dimension to patient care. The innovation attracted nationwide attention. At age thirty-one our hero was named director of electronic data processing.

The glory shot straight to his head. He adopted the notion that his position and power were unassailable and stopped competing to hold them. Having sampled the sweet scent of acclaim, he craved more of the same. He joined organizations left and right, accepted committee chairmanships, became a favored luncheon speaker. He fell into the trap of two- and three-hour "luncheon meetings." Instead of keeping up with the state of his art, he blissfully dozed on Cloud 9.

He gave the matter small thought. Having attained a pinnacle of sorts, he was content to relax and enjoy it. He didn't enjoy it for long. Our hero's chief talent was his ability to tackle and solve complex problems. That was why he had been appointed. But increasingly he delegated problem solving to subordinates. In fact, so skilled did he become at "delegating" whenever a tough challenge presented itself that the outcome was inevitable. In time he delegated himself out of a job.

Corporations often wind up on Cloud 9 because officers are lulled by the belief that success of itself breeds success. If you want evidence, check a June 19, 1971, *Business Week* article entitled "How Kaiser Dug a Hole for Itself." This sad tale of dollar dopeplomacy has its origins high up in the Canadian Rockies (close to the clouds). There "a huge dragline scoops up fifty-four cubic yards of dirt and rock with every pass of its mammoth bucket. Giant shovels bite into seams of coal fifty-feet thick. Massive two-hundred-ton trucks rumble along broad, smooth roads hacked out of primeval wilderness."

Dubbed "Elkview," the ambitious coal-mining operation looks and sounds efficient, but it's not. It's described as "a money-eating monster," costing far more to build and run than its operator, Kaiser Resources, Ltd., and its parent, Kaiser Steel Corp., anticipated. In 1970 a $4.7-million loss was chalked up; in 1971 another $6.4 million went down the drain. On top of this $23 million in start-up costs were earmarked to be written off against subsequent income.

For Kaiser Steel, as *Business Week* reported, Elkview was not only financially painful but embarrassing as well. Before Kaiser Steel became involved, several major corporations, including U.S. Steel, had looked hard at Elkview and turned thumbs down on the project—too remote and inaccessible, too mountainous, not viable.

But Kaiser, intoxicated at the time by its success with the extremely profitable Hamerley Iron mine in Western Australia, decided to dig first and think later. The result was predictable. The project ran into a series of misadventures and unforeseen problems, ranging from management errors and engineering blunders to hassles with customers over the price of the coal. At Elkview everything from geology and weather to equipment and labor turned sour.

At times even the bluest of blue-chip faces turn red on Cloud 9. Long dominant in the cash register market, for years National Cash Register Co. (NCR) also enjoyed a respectable share of the nation's accounting machine business. The quality of its products was second to none, but the company acted too late and too feebly, insiders believe, in response to killer sharks invading its waters.

"NCR awoke with a jolt," notes one analyst, "when red ink splashed over its books in 1972 for the first time since the Great Depression of 1933." It had never occurred to management that the tides could reverse.

Reverse they did, and industry experts fault top management generally and poor product planning specifically. One competitor compares the company to an impregnable fortress on top of a hill in a Latin American country just past the turn of the century. For years, invulnerable to attack from its enemies, its commanding officers grew complacent and smug. A careless vigil was maintained. "Management" saw no need for a roof. In this fashion the years passed by. Then one day a great metal bird flew over, and that was the end of the fort. NCR's blooper was not all that different. You can't argue with long years of success, management believed. The top team considered itself invul: rable. Isolated from the realities of the marketplace, it was ripe for attack.

NCR left itself wide open. It was late bringing important new support products into its computer, cash register, and accounting machine lines. As a consequence it lost ground to competitors. Long-loyal salesmen were angered and demoralized; the company's image was seriously injured.

Today, on the heels of a general computer industry shakeout, a dynamic new president of National Cash Register is hard at work trying to undo what's been done. From recent reports Operation Turnaround is well under way. But it will be years—if ever—before the company can fully recoup its losses stemming from its failures as a result of success.

Less to be faulted, perhaps, is a New York publisher who a few years back got carried away by the success of an author's first book. The situation is common enough. There is a saying in the book publishing business that many a small publisher has been ruined by a best-selling book. In this case the author had produced a spectacular best seller, and his agent coaxed an outrageous advance out of the publisher for his next opus, which was presumably gestating. Today the publisher morosely admits, "I was hypnotized by prospects of another bonanza. He did it once. His name was hot. I assumed his next book would sell equally well."

He should have known better. It is easy enough to point out that the publishing business is an educated gamble at best. You commit yourself to an investment, lose a pile, win a pile, or break even. If you guess more winners than losers, you're ahead of the game.

Well and good, but others disagree and brand the publisher as a Cloud 9 floater. Had his feet been planted more solidly on terra firma, he would have remembered that very few authors are able to repeat an outstanding success. Many writers have only one book to write. In any case the second book is overdue by four years, and the author has no way to repay the advance. All he can do is promise to get started on the second book soon, a promise that has long since begun to pall on the publisher.

From what we have witnessed in our stratospheric meanderings, Cloud 9 euphorics can bust an organization, an individual, or an image. The antidote is simple enough to be missed. Face the stark, no-two-ways-about-it reality that short, easy routes to success don't exist except in rare and freak instances. And as too often happens last season's hero can be next season's bum.

Success is elusive and rich killings are hard to come by, even for the most talented among us. Making it big, from what we can gather, requires a generous portion of imagination and courage, on the one hand, tempered by the thoughtful application of the basics of good business and management, on the other. No substitute we have ever heard of will ever take the place of hard work, realistic analysis, and thoughtful planning every step of the way.

If you score a big success as a manager, more power to you. If you develop a product or service that brings customers fawning, make the most of it. If you engage in a venture that reaps a rich harvest, enjoy it. But keep in mind that what you do *next* can determine the course of your future. The prescription on the heels of success is to check your elevation periodically to make sure you're not floating. If in checking you find that your feet are even two inches off the ground, it is time to take stock.

CHAPTER 19

Nail Noshing

Business, like marriage, is in large part a gamble. But if you marry for the right reasons, there's a fair chance it will work out. And that is also true about business. Decisions, ventures, experiments are—or should be—based on something more than a roll of the dice. The idea is to research, investigate, analyze. In the end you produce a reasoned judgment one way or the other. Right or wrong, at least you make the best use of your training, experience, savvy, and instinct in support of your ideas and convictions. Or do you?

You don't if you're a confirmed nail nosher. When confronted with the need to take a sensible calculated risk, the nail nosher munches away at his fingertips because he lacks the balls to act on his convictions. Either he does that or he avoids forming convictions so that he won't have to face the challenge of supporting them.

This gutless manager worries so much about upsetting the canoe that he remains on shore while the others push off. For him innovation spells danger; yesterday's action is the model for tomorrow. As time passes the nail nosher's canoe doesn't sink, it simply rots away.

At the turn of this decade, according to one press report, a large timberland and lumber company was regarded by analysts as "an impregnable wooden fortress." But as an industry observer wryly noted, "Fortress or not, when dry rot sets in, an organization is in trouble."

What he referred to was the corporation's financial ultraconservatism. It had no long-term debt at a time when major competitors were launching ambitious expansion plans. Its balance sheet showed cash holdings equal to 20 percent of stockholders' equity. It displayed lackluster growth that had shareholders fuming. Defending its do-nothing policy, a top executive said, "We sleep better at night." To which a wag replied, "Yes, and in the daytime too."

When a marriage bogs down, it usually takes drastic action to revive it. That can also be true of a corporation, institution, or government agency. Not so very long ago a major aerospace producer found itself losing altitude rapidly. The cause was directly traceable to a team of nail-noshing top executives. For years the company had relied on government orders as the mainstay of its business. But with direct involvement of American troops in Viet Nam at an end— despite heavy U.S. funding of South Viet Nam's war machine in the continuing combat—orders were no longer sufficient to sustain the company's payroll and plant. Sales shriveled to a fraction of what the volume had been in the sixties.

Yet the corporation had developed great technological prowess, had excellent plant and facilities, and had an outstanding complement of talented engineers and other professionals. "The time was long overripe," says one analyst, "for this company to develop new products and markets. Rockwell and others have done it and emerged as healthy, viable organizations as a result."

What was wrong? Was management waiting for another war to get the plant's engine revved up again? It's a tough question to answer; decision paralysis never is easily explained. Whatever the case, when the company's top brass weren't busy noshing their nails, they were sitting on their hands.

Nail noshing tends to undermine not only organizations but individuals as well. A chief executive in the petroleum products industry hired a bright young administrative assistant with advanced degrees well embroidered with ivy. The young man was personable and articulate and had a stratospheric IQ. He had been in the top 1 percent of his class. Clearly executive material, and with long-term grooming in mind, the chief had a high post in mind for him.

This corporate leader, an admirer of former president John F. Kennedy, used aides and other subordinates as sounding boards for his ideas and views. With his new assistant's obvious mental equipment the boss figured he would be ideal for this purpose. It didn't work out as planned. In response to the chief's, "Well, what do you think?" the young man was rarely without comment. He chipped in with tidbits here and there that were bright and discerning. But they were always in favor, always in support; he never seemed to disagree.

Now the corporate head was no fool. No one knew better than he that in this business game of "Decision Roulette," you can't always, or nearly always, be right. If you wind up batting 600 or thereabouts, you are doing quite well. On the other hand, he made allowances for his assistant's tender age and experience. Conceivably the aide could be overwhelmed and overawed by his boss and for that reason not question his judgment. So the chief decided to put his new assistant to the test. He concocted a plan that was basically unsound, so unsound that an individual of lesser intelligence readily would have pinpointed its weakness. Outlining the plan he asked for his assistant's opinion. Again, the young man responded with what appeared to be thoughtful consideration. He came up with a few minor, harmless suggestions and was bright and articulate as usual. He also fairly quivered with sincerity. But as his boss noted with a sigh, he had not a word to express in opposition to the idea presented. He lacked the courage to assert his own viewpoint or stand up to the boss. The incident dispelled any shadow of doubt that remained. However bright this recruit might be, the chief decided, his principal talent was his acting ability. It was a talent that was of very little help to him on the day he was fired.

The courage to develop and fight for convictions, and meet head on the inevitable risk of innovation and change, is as crucial to this nation's institutions and agencies as it is to its industrial enterprises. Nail noshing defeats all kinds of objectives—social, financial, or whatever.

One of America's best-known secretarial schools, for decades prestigious and profitable, has been sliding downhill in recent years. It has become known for its staid and stuffy approach and its refusal to respond aggressively to the accelerating change of the seventies. So impressed is this institution's fusty top executive with his organization's seemingly unassailable status, it apparently has not occurred to him that today's pressing demands for reform and restructuring could apply to him also. Each year, the school's programs are growing more outdated and less responsive to the demands of a society in transition. As a result it has been losing ground steadily to smaller but more progressive competitors. Outstanding among these is the fast-growing Berkeley Secretarial School.

Berkeley's dynamic young academic dean, Jo Ann Joyner, explains the school's increasing popularity among career-minded young women. "Responsiveness," she maintains, "is the operational word. It's a matter of identifying needs—student needs, teacher needs, prospective employer needs, and making moves to fulfill them. Making moves implies change, and change implies risk," she concedes. "But in this field, at least, there is more risk in not making moves."

Jo Ann Joyner could be talking about almost any field. When the productivity bungler in his nail-noshing trance resists inevitable trends and does battle with progress, he invites deterioration and decline.

The philosophy is simple. When realities become clear, it makes sense to confront them head on.

Reality number one for any secretarial school deals with the growing independence and determination of the liberated woman to step into her rightful place in professional management when trained and qualified to do so. Progress in this direction, however slow, is inevitable. Ambitious, intelligent, career-minded women are moving—and proving themselves—in areas of leadership and management that were almost exclusively male in dark ages past. Innovative and imaginative educational institutions keep in touch with this and other trends by maintaining continuous contact with both prospective employers and graduates.

"Their needs complement each other," Dean Joyner explains. "The response virtually dictates itself in terms of a well-rounded program of management-geared courses that sharpen professional and managerial skills well beyond such mundane secretarial fare as typing and shorthand."

Other schools are following Berkeley's bold leadership. But except for a handful what they offer is mainly lip service to women's march on industry. The right labels have been affixed to the programs, but the programs lack honest depth. The schools lack the courage to initiate the kind of radical change that pays off in recognition and growth. Prospective employers react negatively, and so do the students.

The educator James Conant summed it up in a nutshell when he said, "Behold the turtle. He makes progress only when he sticks his neck out."

In short, you get the richest and ripest fruit by going out on a limb. This is no pitch for reckless risk taking. But in today's highly competitive, rapidly changing environment, as Dean Joyner points out, reasoned and sensible risk taking, grounded on knowledge, experience, and analysis, is often less risky than burrowing your head in the sand or nibbling your nails right down to the flesh.

CHAPTER 20

Reckless Driving

We can pinpoint, in general, four types of corporate entity. One is the operation that's sliding—behind its competitors and behind the times. Then there's the outfit that bumbles along on a fairly steady plateau—neither growing nor losing, more or less status quo. A third is the dynamic, fast-moving company that experiments and innovates, pioneers new ideas, and explores opportunities aggressively but with good sense and care. Number four is the supercharged, go-and-grow organization that can't move fast enough or make money enough to satisfy the hungry demands of its chief. To accelerate growth, management races the corporate engine, recklessly driving its people beyond reasonable limits in the process.

The example that comes to mind is a Midwestern mini-conglomerate that grew too big for its britches and split them. This company's chairman is a smart ex-financial executive in his thirties. A clever, persuasive promoter, he started modestly enough, buying into and eventually taking over a parts manufacturer doing $500,000 in sales per year. Restless and impatient, he acquired four small subsidiaries and consolidated operations. His timing and judgment were good.

The business grew, and so, in turn, did his ego. He

hired a ghost writer who listened to him spout management wisdom and philosophy and then penned deathless prose about how to succeed. With his second book published, the chief believes he has now truly *arrived* and is qualified to instruct IBM, Xerox, and GM on how it ought to be done.

About a year and a half ago the nation's Gift to Big Business decided (soundly enough) that he needed a sophisticated computer installation to control his increasingly far-flung and diversified interests. He hired a computer expert and set him up as electronic data processing manager. Suppliers were contacted, a computer system selected, and a proposal laid out at a meeting of the supplier's rep, his district supervisor, the corporate controller, the computer expert, and the chairman himself.

"When can we get the system on stream?" the chief wanted to know.

The rep replied, "It will take at least fourteen months from the date of the order to get the program checked out and running."

"You have to be kidding!"

The chief was stubborn, intractable. Fourteen months was out of the question, he insisted. His plan called for nine months or less.

The data processing manager, looking worried, cut in. He explained about the planning, staffing, training, programming, and debugging. "It's impossible."

"Nothing's impossible if you set your mind to the task."

The rep tried to reason with him, but he refused to back down. It was nine months or else.

"Or else" meant no order. The salesman's superior chimed in, "We can do it if we have to."

The rep moistened his lips. The electronic data processing manager maintained a numb silence. The contract was signed.

You know the rest of the story. The manager and his

staff worked all kinds of hours and programmed their hearts out. But the goal was unrealistic; it couldn't be met. In the end applications were put on stream prematurely; the mess was prodigious—it was a colossal nonsystem. The data processing manager resigned to preserve what health and sanity he had left. The fiasco cost a sickening sum and almost ruined the company.

Pressure that drives men beyond reasonable limits can run both the men and the enterprise down, whether the enterprise be public or private. We should have learned this lesson decades ago, but apparently haven't. In England, well over a half-century ago forty-four lives were lost when a government-built airship, the R.38, broke in two and burst into flames during a trial flight. In his book, *Slide Rule,* author and air industry pioneer Nevil Shute tells how, with this tragedy fresh in its mind, the government, wishing to continue the airship program, ruled that "the Air Ministry at Cardington shall build an airship of a certain size, load-carrying capacity, and speed, and Vickers, Ltd., shall build another one to the same contract specifications." It was government versus private enterprise, with fierce competition between the two groups developing. In such an environment cooperation and communications weren't easy to come by.

Despite limited financial resources and all kinds of hardships the Vickers-built R.100, carefully checked and doublechecked every step of the way, proved successful in all of its tests. The crew was made up of efficient, dedicated, and highly competent administrators and technologists.

The government-built R.101 was another story entirely. As Shute, who was deputy chief engineer of the R.100, explained in his book:

> An airship is safe in proportion to its useful lift, in proportion to the weights that it can jettison in an emergency, and by that standard R.101 was definitely dangerous. . . . The design seemed to us (the R.100 crew) almost unbelievably complicated; she seemed to be a ship in which imagination had run

riot regardless of the virtue of simplicity and utterly regardless of expense.

Among innumerable problems and deficiencies were leaking gas valves, chafing gasbags, and a defective outer cover.

When the time of its scheduled test flight to India drew close, worried members of the R.101 group requested postponement and succeeded in delaying the flight briefly. But additional requests for delay were not received kindly, partly due to the R.100 group's announcement that it was ready to make its own scheduled test flight to Canada. This tightened the competitive screws. Further pressure on the R.101 people was exerted by the Air Ministry's drum-beating press corps, who repeatedly crowed to the world that the R.101 was a flawless and superior ship.

But the roughest pressure of all was created by the program's supreme commander, Britain's Secretary of State for Air Lord Christopher Birdwood Thomson, a politician with a high personal career stake in the R.101's success, a stake that might have been thwarted by any hitch in the program. As late as three weeks before the disaster, noted Shute, in response to increasing pressures the R.101 group was "floundering, making hurried and incompetent technical decisions, excluding people from their conferences who could have helped them." A short preliminary test flight was made, but it was made under ideal weather conditions and not at full speed.

On October 4, 1930, the R.101 set out for India. Bad weather and high winds developed rapidly, so that the only safe and sane course would have been to turn back. But Lord Thomson himself was on board, and turning back would have injured his political program. The airship crashed over France, killing forty-seven persons, including Lord Thomson.

Large sums of money as well as human life can be lost when people are forced under pressure to launch programs or products prematurely. Engineers in a New England company came up with an ingeniously designed multipurpose pump. Specs were reviewed and found faultless. A consultant confirmed this opinion. Marketing got carried away with enthusiasm. The profit potential was exciting. And then came the screws.

The president asked, "How long will it take for the working model to be developed and perfected?"

The chief engineer was reluctant to be pinned down. "It's impossible to predict," he explained. "You never know what you'll run into."

The president pressed for a date and finally got one. "Maybe six to eight months."

The boss whittled this down to five to six months. A marketing program was set up which included advertising, distribution, selling, promotion—the works. The president was on the engineer's back daily. "How's it going? How's it going?" Said the engineer later, "I heard those words in my sleep. If we failed to meet that deadline, I was sure it would cost me my job."

After a fashion the deadline was met, but it required compromising with standards and tolerances. Notes one industry observer, "That pump had all the potential predicted, but it was introduced prematurely."

The ads claimed it could be run dry without damage. Unfortunately that claim didn't hold up. It was too noisy in operation and less efficient than promised. Thousands of pumps were sold, and many hundreds returned. The company lost $1 million on the product plus incalculable damage to its reputation.

Accountability for results is one of the foremost of management basics. Attempting accountability for the unachievable can burn out the corporate engine swiftly. In a major food products company a new breakfast cereal involved a tremendous development and advertising investment. The product manager, edged far out on a limb, had a crucial stake in the item's success. His career virtually hinged on the outcome. Understandably he touted the new cereal as the most exciting product to hit the market since Wheaties. Many customers didn't share this assessment.

One chain store executive's reaction was typical. He didn't think the cereal would catch on in his area and refused to yield the shelf and display space requested. The product manager, responding to pressures from above, was insistent.

As the temperature heated, the product manager dropped polite pretenses. He had ways of forcing compliance, which involved warehousing and trucking arrangements, and spelled these out for the customer. For one thing he could refuse chain store trucks access to supplier warehouses along regular routes, meaning they would have to "deadhead"—return empty—one way.

The customer had no choice but to swallow his anger and pride and agree to give in. The pressure worked superficially but caused more harm than good. Store managers went through the motions as instructed. But the word filtered through. Help was negligent in stacking, displaying, and pricing the product; promotion material was lost or discarded; competitive products were pushed. In the end the cereal failed miserably.

One store manager observed acidly, "They would have had to keep a man on hand as a permanent lookout to get what they wanted."

Pressure levels tend to stratify and build in large corporations. The magic word is performance, and for the supercharged manager individual performance is tied more to tomorrow than yesterday. Whatever last month's results next month's must always shine brighter in terms of sales, productivity, and profits—sometimes unreasonably so.

In a large textile products company's Eastern division a cold-eyed quality control manager, newly installed, had heady dreams for his future. Damaged goods, in the cutting department in particular, had been excessive for months. The new man, as his title implied, had been hired to bring quality under control. In so doing he attacked the problem but neglected the cause.

Hows and whys didn't matter, he let his people know. What he wanted was results. There's nothing wrong with wanting results if your goal is realistic and you shoot for it in a rational way. This tactless task manager didn't follow this line. Instead of probing to learn *why* the reject rate was excessive, he tried to browbeat foremen and supervisors into flawless performances. He didn't take the time to do the job right. He wanted instant success.

What he got was instant failure. First, the zero-rejects goal he tried to set was absurd. His favorite credo was, "One bad piece of work is one piece too many." He had posters made up with this axiom and plastered them all over the plant.

One day he found a poster turned around, the following legend written on its back: "One piece of lousy treatment is one piece too many."

It defined the core of the problem. However poor the reject rate, employee morale was even worse. Workers were underpaid, poorly treated, made to feel like machines. Quality control had as much meaning and interest for them as the price of beans in North Borneo. Yet the manager kept hammering away at performance and pressured supervisors to the point where he convinced them their jobs were on the line if the reject rate didn't drop dramatically.

It dropped dramatically enough on paper. Inevitably a new system evolved. Instead of being reported as rejects, damaged goods were carted out with the trash. The quality control chief became a hero overnight. Then, when inventory shortages were discovered, undercover investigators revealed the true cause. The result was a massive shake-up, during which our supercharged friend was shaken loose from his job.

Sometimes corporate engines—and engineers—are recklessly driven by executive pile drivers seeking to hammer their way into the marketplace. In his book, *Mismarketing,*

Thomas L. Berg tells how Rheingold strived to dominate the West Coast beer market in the early fifties. Looking for new worlds to conquer, the company disregarded regional preferences and the complex reasons why consumers remain loyal to particular brands. While attempting to blitz Western markets, promotion in their established market was neglected, resulting in drastic slippage at home and the eventual sale of the Rheingold breweries. As one prominent observer noted, "You simply can't ram any brand you wish down a beer drinker's throat. Nor can you run counter to the natural trends of an industry."

In another situation a leading cosmetics maker, swooning from past fragrance and lipstick conquests, developed a unique beauty treatment spray product. Adopting a Midas touch, we-can-do-nothing-wrong attitude, the chief executive insisted that the item be introduced to the market on a specified date, despite the remonstrances of the chief chemist, production manager, and other executives that the product still needed work and that production wheels couldn't be set into motion quickly enough to meet the unrealistic deadline. Impatiently brushing aside this "negative thinking," the president, in a rush to beat competitors to market, mandated that the spray be introduced prematurely after superficial tests. The result was calamitous to earnings, prestige, and not least of all morale. The chief chemist, nerves frazzled and raw from the ordeal, sought and found a lucrative post with one of the competitors the president had sought to beat out. Other managers remained but were embittered by the experience. The spray worked well for the first thirty or forty days of its life. But after that it gummed up, the consistency failed to hold, and many units stopped working entirely. Customer complaints and returns avalanched. Today the president glumly concedes, "It was the biggest bath we ever took."

Horace once said, "The covetous man is ever in want." Reckless driving motivated by greed very rarely pays off.

The thirst for power has a way of intoxicating faster

than alcohol and often spurs reckless driving. The most destructive form of reckless driving may be the result of super-egotism—the vain and arrogant contention that "the black cat is green if I say so." The superegotist is so enchanted with his magic power that he gives little thought to whether what he wants to happen is realistically achievable.

Superegotist Napoleon once said, "Impossible is a word only to be found in the dictionary of fools." He found it in Russia and at Waterloo as well.

We have no argument with the positive approach when it is applied with reasoned thought and humanity. When it is mindlessly exercised in a way that exerts killing pressures on people, the reckless driver may find that he's headed for his own personal Waterloo.

CHAPTER 21

Deadwood Preservation

How does bureaucracy breed incompetence? The answer is simple enough—the system feeds on itself. Typically the new organization starts off lean, tight, and purposeful. But as it grows in size the work spreads out. Key men hire aides, and the aides hire aides. The layers multiply and flourish.

Unwittingly a change in organizational life-style takes place. It's what Roger Lemelin ran into when he took over *La Presse,* previously Quebec's largest-circulation French-language newspaper. Lemelin, Canada's best-known author, is also an astute businessman, who once parlayed a $50,000 investment in a meat-packing enterprise into a $2.5-million property.

When he assumed control of *La Presse,* the once highly profitable operation was sagging, the productivity rate low. The new chief found employees "working in a tomb." After Lemelin stepped into the top job, the ailing enterprise was restored to its number one spot. His first day on the job, the story goes, eleven members of senior management who weren't carrying their weight were in at 11 A.M. and out by noon—with generous severance pay checks.

One editor recalls, "Before Lemelin, *La Presse* was

organized to administer a company like General Motors. We were always speaking to the assistant to the vice president's assistant."

Particularly prone to layerism and the entrenchment of submarginal performers is the family-owned company. A medium-size parts manufacturer is tottering on the edge of bankruptcy in these tough times of inflation-recession. One insider sourly reveals it is top-heavy with "aunts, uncles, and cousins you can reckon by the dozens." Another says, "There are six fancy titles to go with every management function—and some functions that are largely nonfunctional." With troubles piling on troubles, an industry observer characterizes the company as "one big unhappy family."

Recently, at a top-level meeting, one of the brothers brought up the problem of his son Melvin, a college dropout. According to Pop, Melvin is a "good boy. All he needs is a chance." The problem was finding a place where Melvin could fit into the business. In view of the company's financial troubles Pop reluctantly agreed to start him at a relatively low-level job in the production department. The decision triggered a family brouhaha, with wives and aunts getting into the act. To restore family harmony Melvin is now "a manager." But if things continue as they have been lately, he may soon have nothing to manage.

When the roster becomes larded with managers who don't manage and supervisors who don't supervise, organizations become devitalized to the very edge of extinction. Managerial titles are a good deal like cockroaches. Once established in residence and allowed to proliferate, it takes more than DDT to get rid of them.

A team of management analysts was brought in some years ago in an effort to learn why so many managerial foul-ups were occurring at the middle and high-middle echelons of a major airline and why the organization had veered millions of dollars off its profit course. A key factor, according to the probers' report, was that "management is top-heavy and unwieldy. It has lost its capacity to react fast enough to opportunities and problems." The public-relations department, split and subdivided all over the place, was cited as an example. "Five years ago," the report explained, "one vice president was in charge of a main function or responsibility and he clearly knew how to lead. Today the same job is handled by two or three senior VPs with four junior VPs reporting to them, and nobody understands what is happening."

Too often a manager's status is measured more by his personal sphere of influence than by the job that he does. As a result a subtle conversion from "doer" to "operator" takes place. With lieutenants bearing the workload, the need to "stay abreast" diminishes. The temptation to yield to the easy competence-eroding life grows stronger.

Too many managers take Andrew Carnegie's famous counsel to heart, "The great manager is the man who knows how to surround himself with men much abler than himself." They interpret this to mean, "Hire subordinates who are smart enough to relieve you of the responsibility of thinking, planning, and managing."

Consciously or not, when a manager starts down this path, he's taken the first sliding step toward incompetence. As his competence fades a new problem confronts him: how to justify his existence in order to perpetuate his job. So he dreams up nonproductive productions, complex studies and surveys, and elaborate projects and programs. The truly creative lardee is adept at concocting all kinds of intriguing experiments under the sacred umbrella of innovation and change.

Take reports as an example. We have become a nation of infomaniacs, producing information for the sake of producing information. We grind out mountains of reports and analyses that all too often tell us in well-chronicled detail a good deal about nothing significant.

When the population of semicompetents grows excessive in the nonprofit organization, the brunt of the problem is borne by the taxpayer and consumer, who foots the tab in the end. As the ranks swell, costs proliferate, along with inefficiency. Most commonly the institution's or agency's simple response is to put in for increased funding, which is traditionally based more on numbers than results. As the organization mushrooms, the chief cooks increase in importance, and everyone's happy.

In commercial enterprise it's a different story entirely. The profit-geared business can tolerate only so much nonproductivity and larding. When costs exceed revenues, stockholders growl, and board members respond. The result is organizational shake-up. A new top team takes over. Operation Turnaround gets under way.

But disentrenching the incompetents and supernumeraries is no simple matter, as at least one large oil company can confirm from experience. Headquartered in Oklahoma, where the company employs 15 percent of the town's population of 35,000, after three years of sliding profits a complete structural revamping took place. A skilled managerial surgeon was brought in to perform the critically needed organizectomy. What he found was managerial and supervisory nonproducers crowding the beach like Sunday bathers at Coney Island.

The destaffing was done as it had to be done. But in a close-knit company, where everyone knows everyone personally, this was a stunt to pull off. Executives ordered to streamline their operations received calls at home from wailing wives. "How can you do this to Jim?"

The need isn't easy to explain to a distraught woman. Vows the new chief, "I view the task of making sure we never get into a spot like this again to be one of my highest priorities."

The seasoned head of a nationally known management-consulting firm, after helping a client through an unsettling organizational shake-up, was heard to grumble at a majority stockholder, "I think I've finally hit on the magic formula to ensure corporate success and well-being. Fire every vice president and upgrade his assistant. Do this every five years, and you'll wind up a leader in your industry."

Half jest or not, it's a disquieting thought. From some of the productivity mayhem we've observed in executive suites, it may not be so harebrained as it sounds.

A large federal agency had grown unwieldy, inefficient, and semifunctional over a period of years—so much so that it had become a prime target for journalists and Naderists. Inevitably when the odor ripened, an audit took place. It revealed shocking duplication and waste, three- and four-hour-long lunch periods, and costly junkets by "research and study" groups equipped with open minds and full golfing regalia.

One administrator even confessed to running a small business on the side, devoting incidental effort to agency affairs. On the heels of the report major surgery was applied. The payroll was slashed, jobs and functions realigned, and unessential tasks defined and eliminated. In the end operating costs were chopped almost in half.

It must be stated that most personnel in this agency were dedicated, honorable, and hard-working public servants. One manager, asked how the organization could have been permitted to deteriorate so shamefully, replied honestly enough, "I guess we were never before pressured into rooting out the deadwood."

Rooting out the deadwood, the noncontributing free riders, can breathe new life into a drowning organization. A medium-size college, successful for over a century, one day found itself heading for Rocksville. Registration was down, and student and faculty esprit little more than a sham. The president couldn't say for sure that six months hence the payroll would be met.

A savvy financial executive was recruited in an effort to save this once venerable institution. Department by department he ferreted through the school, examining functions and jobs under a high-powered lens. He found what he expected to find, layer on layer of fat, with scores of noncontributors "carried" on the payroll. "In one section," he notes, "a thirty-two-thousand-dollar-a-year general was running the show; a twenty-five-thousand-dollar colonel was running his errands; a thirteen-thousand-dollar sergeant was doing the work. I got rid of the brass, promoted the sergeant to captain, and saved more than fifty thousand dollars a year." Today he gets the job done faster, more efficiently, and with less red tape.

Ask any manager what chore he dreads most. Almost invariably his answer will be, "Firing a subordinate."

Granted, the firing task is, at best, hardly a joyous event. But neither need it be the agony most managers make of it. Realistically viewed, if an employee must be severed because he's not carrying his weight, the best favor you can do for the organization, yourself, *and most likely for him* is to focus on the positive aspects of the situation.

A handful of incompetents can clog up the works faster than sand poured in a watch. By its very nature bureaucracy tends to breed a certain number of incompetents within each working group, and a close look at most organizations will reveal more than a handful.

At the head of the list is the employee who seems to be allergic to his company, his boss, or his job. The bitter, frustrated employee works counter to organizational objectives and usually his own goals as well. His continued employment is a detriment to all concerned, most of all to himself. If he is totally beyond salvation, firing him will be a kindness. He really wants to be released.

Then there's the marginal performer who would like to do better but lacks the ability to do so. As we have seen, unrealistic goals create unnatural tensions. Chances are that this poor fellow, straining like the devil to perform beyond his level of competence, is doing himself physical and psychical damage. Keeping him on may sustain his present income, while jeopardizing his outcome at exorbitant cost to both the organization and the man.

The most difficult person to fire is the experienced, dedicated, once-qualified employee who is no longer qualified because of automation, loss of business, or change of direction or plan. Still he remains larded on the payroll, the responsibility he once enjoyed replaced with a mess of busy work. As his status erodes, so does his self-respect and the respect of his peers. What's more, the older he gets, the more out of date he becomes, and the more unemployable. As hard field experience bears out, keeping your competent supernumeraries on the payroll is no act of friendship.

Despite the realities the human tendency is for many managers to defer the firing decision. Doing so leads to all kinds of problems. In a fiberboard plant it led to a crippling strike that should have been anticipated but wasn't. One day without warning machines ground to a halt, trucks stopped rolling, and orders piled up to the crossbeams while customers howled. Reason: an intractable, hard-headed labor relations vice president who still lived in the thirties had bungled a minor shop flare-up. Nobody wanted the strike, least of all labor. But with the fuse touched off, face had to be saved.

"This issue is negotiable," a tight-lipped shop steward told management finally, "but not until that man is out of the picture."

The problem once pinpointed was no surprise to the general manager, who knew the vice president harbored archaic notions about the vested rights of management. Having surrounded himself with a small empire of his own, the VP was effectively insulated from reality. After he was fired, the situation returned to normal. But as his boss ruefully concedes, the action was long overdue.

As experience testifies, the less nonproductive and counterproductive bodies on hand to clutter up the office or shop, the better efficiency you achieve, the less paper you see shuffled from in-box to in-box, the less meetings are called, the fewer committees set up, the more meaningful work gets accomplished. When the tierocracy slims down to its right level of competence, action multiplies, problems get tackled and solved faster, and decisions are made more effectively.

CHAPTER 22

Team-Busting Tactics

A toy-manufacturing company recently moved from the heart of a New England town to its outskirts. The new plant was only partially air conditioned. Transportation was inconvenient. More important, employees had been given only four weeks notice. They were neither consulted about the move nor given preliminary briefings. Morale took a dive. A third of the company's 1,800 employees quit, including almost a fifth of its supervisory work force.

In a ninety-personnel city administration, employee problems appeared to be brewing. A management consultant suggested an attitude survey to track down the source of the trouble. His suggestion was mulled over and discussed. But the city manager put off taking action. It was a relatively small group, he decided. He was certain he knew how everyone felt. When the lit fuse inevitably touched powder, he realized how wrong he had been. Productivity plummeted. Absenteeism shot up. Turnover multiplied. When the survey was finally made, shocking disclosures about true employee feelings almost triggered the manager's nervous collapse. Workers were disgruntled by supervisory autocracy, resentful over broken promises about training opportunities, and bitter about rigid Army-type work rules and a host of other things.

In a Midwestern wholesale operation the executive vice president opted for early retirement. The chief executive, hastily and with no apparent preparation, named one of three senior VPs to the spot. Assuming that the move ruled them out of the presidential succession race, the other two quit.

A big government agency computerized part of its operation without consulting its people or properly preparing them for the conversion. People resigned in droves. The system almost broke down.

Delays, omissions, and impulsive, ill-pondered actions of this type are costing private and public organizations a mint. When arrangements take place that make significant changes which do not take account of human responses or which blithely take it for granted that harmony prevails in the ranks, without taking the pulse, it's fairly begging for trouble.

A classic example is the ongoing hassle over managerial transfers. I recently heard a bull-headed senior executive growl, "Hell, in this outfit we don't ask a man if he wants to be transferred, we transfer him. If he goes along, fine, it's a boost. If he balks, he's either out on his butt or told that he's reached his plateau."

Three cheers for this battle-scarred general. He's losing the war but preserving his image. Within the ranks he is fostering rancor that will return to thwart management objectives for years to come.

Many IBMers you chat with will remember the time when a joke circulating around the company wryly explained that IBM stands for "I've been moved." The message had a clarion ring. In those days mobility meant advancement, refusal dead end.

In more recent years IBM's top planners have thoughtfully reassessed the company's transfer philosophy. Opinion polls reveal how people truly feel. In many cases if transfer means promotion, it is fervently sought. But where youngsters are involved, managers are likely to have disquieting second thoughts. As IBM's high brass concedes, anxieties over the impact of too-frequent moves on the lives of small children can be valid indeed. It's new grist for the decision-making mill, and so is the individual's right to weigh career factors against family considerations on a scale that doesn't assign deific privileges to the Corporate High Command. In short, a manager's reluctance to pull up his roots and resettle is no longer the supreme act of subordinate defiance.

This sounds to me like good news. Maybe—just maybe —a handful of managers nationwide are becoming more human. Hopefully they're recognizing that the real key to this diamond-studded chalice of Improved Productivity we all so heroically crusade for lies in an employee's attitude about his job, his boss, his company. And maybe some managers are beginning to appreciate that the factors shaping this attitude are as fragile as a matchstick castle.

Bravo! But it's no reason to get all choked up. Let's not delude ourselves. Armies of blunder-prone profit poopers are still dreaming up innumerable ploys to undermine team effort. Nor are they about to cease and desist. For its sobering value take a quick peek into their little chest of sharp and jagged tools.

* Make it hard for your people to bring you their problems.
* Permit minor complaints to fester into boils of disloyalty.
* Don't bother to inform or consult with your people about crucial decisions that affect their lives.
* Wound employee pride with rude inattention, interruptions, and a general lack of respect while in conversation with them.
* Snow people with bureaucratic double-talk when they make suggestions or register gripes.

How Sure Fail can you get? Are tactics like these on the ebb? Much as I'd like to say yes, I seriously doubt it. I see too much evidence of management's blasé response to the attitudes of people. Enter any organization where this is prevalent and pierce the outer shell of superficial relationships; underneath you will probably find a deep rancor brewing.

Anyone who follows the current press closely will be easily convinced that a sizzling new trend has been launched. Top managers, he'll conclude, are as busy as little red ants honing their sensitivities to the way people feel. Scads of corporate helmsmen are scrambling from their inner sanctums to hobnob with the commoners. In some cases strides have been made. But the sad reality is that most such reports stem not from executive suites but from sweet-singing executives and from professional speech writers and image-fabricating mills. It's the old familiar song and dance designed to shape a sexier corporate profile, boost recruitment efforts, and give community relations a much-needed shot in the tail.

In all fairness, however, sparks of hope are clearly igniting. A fistful of progressive managements are making an honest attempt to zero in on employee feelings. Experiments of this type are worth noting. At General Electric Co. (GE), for example, about 2,000 supervisors attend training sessions geared to make individuals more responsive to their jobs. The goal is to win cooperation through persuasion and participation rather than clobbering tactics. In one GE plant a productivity boost of 20 percent was attributed to this program.

General Foods Corp.'s pet food division in Topeka, Kansas, is another example. There, unsupervised employee teams, freed from time clock restrictions, set their own work goals and schedules. They make hiring and firing decisions and work with management to plan operating techniques. It is reported by GF that the job gets done with a smaller work force than ordinarily required. In an industry where 10 percent absence is the norm, only 1 percent is tallied in this operation. And employee resignations are virtually nonexistent.

TRW, Inc., has been pioneering "job enrichment" and organization development for a decade or more, promoting job interest and fulfillment—in short, expanding human capabilities where possible. The payoff is in projects completed faster and more efficiently, better morale, and increased idea output. As one spokesman puts it, "We're convinced that in terms of productivity the man who is most productive is the one who has a real piece of the action."

Here and there similar experiments are in force with good results. It is an encouraging sign, but bear in mind that reported trends can be misleading. A rash of articles appears, and the assumption takes hold that we're well on our way to a bright and blissful tomorrow. But the reality persists that a handful of forward-thinking organizations don't comprise an economy. Whatever advances have been made, it's still a granule in the rice bucket. Our accustomed failures to communicate still exist. Time-grooved practices that treat people like numbers and try to club them psychologically into compliance are no less prevalent today than they were a decade or two ago. Managers intoxicated by their own self-importance tend to take action first and ponder the consequences later.

In one corporate power feud, conflict between a textile maker's presumably retired chairman-founder and his successor demoralized employees right down the line. With two strong-willed leaders at the helm no one was sure who was really the boss. The twin captains often worked at cross purposes, the orders of one countermanded by the other, the reactions of the crew disregarded. As a result team spirit sagged. Managers, choosing up sides, spent more time on politics than on getting the job done.

However beset we may be with technological advances, human nature isn't likely to change. You can't kick the stuffings out of employee sensitivities and expect people to run an efficient operation in the process. At key management levels, in particular, the smart strategy is to gauge human reaction before making your move.

This applies to the pygmies as well as to the giants. In a small family-owned health care institution plagued by high costs and operating inefficiencies, a bright young executive was appointed administrator. He did a first-rate restructuring job, rooting out duplication and waste and upgrading patient service and employee morale. Within ten months gains were impressive; the institution appeared to be on its way to recovery. But the new administrator made the fatal mistake of locking horns with the man who had hired him. Stomping hard on his chief's ego, he made key decisions without bothering to consult him. He would perfunctorily agree with his boss and then ignore his wishes. The president became increasingly disgruntled. When the administrator made one such blunder too many, he was fired in a fit of rage.

It makes little difference if you are dealing with a clerical employee, supervisor, vice president, or the top man himself; disregarding sensitivities can be dangerous. For any team to excel—a playing team or a working team—individual members require a sufficient measure of self-esteem and respect to develop the kind of attitude and self-confidence from which excellence stems. Franklin Delano Roosevelt said that if civilization is to survive, we must cultivate the science of human relationships. Since organizations are the building blocks of civilization and the teams that run them the builders, it follows that dealing intelligently, sensitively, and compassionately with every player on the team is the only truly sure-win way to wind up at the top of the league.

CHAPTER 23

The Dismal Disincentives

During World War II the Department of Defense dispensed thousands of "E for Excellence" awards to contractors who achieved outstanding performance. Employees wore "Pride" buttons with pride, and "E" banners and stickers were prominently displayed throughout the nation's offices and plants. Inspired out of patriotism and concern for fighting forces abroad, the motivational programs were highly successful. People worked hard to surpass the performance of past periods, even though it meant no personal gain. A similar spirit was seen during the Apollo space program. Fired by the excitement and drama of a massive national effort to land a man on the moon, the world's eyes upon them, employees were motivated to shoot for high levels of achievement without asking, "What's in it for me?"

Some motivation careerists, dazzled by results of this kind, like to think that all it takes to make productivity rocket is to whip workers into a fervor as a college coach revs up his team. They are living for the most part in a never-never dreamland. What moves human spirits during exceptional times of national emergency or endeavor leaves people yawning under ordinary day-to-day circumstances. Locker room pep talks will never take the place of honest incentives. Dispensing crumbs when people want bread is as transparent as a newly cleaned window.

The PR and personnel departments of a Pittsburgh metal products company pooled talents to concoct an elaborate inspirational program designed to bolster sagging performance in office and plant. At the hub of the campaign was a profit booster competition for individual employees and departments. Posters stressing the importance of profits were hung all over the place. Propaganda on quality, productivity, and pride was distributed to workers. The rules of the contest were simple. A management committee using various performance gauges—such as production, number of rejects, and attendance—would select the department and individual in each department contributing most to corporate profits each month. The winning department would get a banner proclaiming it "Profit Booster of the Month." Winning employees would get a plaque with their name inscribed on it, along with a write-up in the company magazine. The overall grand winner would receive an invitation from the president for him and his family to dine at his home.

Employee reaction to the contest and its prizes could be summed up in two words: "Big deal!" In response to the contest marginal performance declined even lower. Sarcastic comments were scribbled over posters and contest announcements. Winners were held in scorn by coworkers. Never had an attempt at productivity improvement so eloquently flopped.

The point makes itself. Locker room motivation rarely works outside the locker room. Employees are no longer naive. Today, people who work for a living—just like corporate executives, investors, and government officials—want to know above all, "What's in it for me?"

It doesn't always have to be money alone, although a fair wage encompasses far more than the cash involved: status for one, self-respect for another. Someone once quipped, "There are things more important than money. The trouble is you need money to buy them."

The reality remains—more so than ever today with purchasing power squeezed by inflation—that a decent wage is a powerful motivator. That doesn't mean it's the *only* motivator—people respond as well to interesting and meaningful work, humane treatment, or a feeling of importance and belonging. But don't sell that old green stuff short.

What it boils down to is that people need honest and genuine incentives to induce them to give their all for The Organization.

Take the Wisconsin machine maker whose compensation experts dreamed up a retirement package that traps employees more and more as their seniority builds. Here, top brass cash in on a generous profit-sharing plan. Supervisors and middle managers bring home turkeys at Christmas and good pensions after thirty years of service. But the price they pay for their old-age security is incalculable. The company's electronic data processing manager is a case in point. An eleven-year veteran, the equity in his retirement fund—money he'd lose if he quit—keeps him tied to a job that robs him of dignity and self-respect. His salary comes to $14,000 a year—plus the turkey. No one knows better than he that with his training and experience he should be earning $20,000 or more. Periodically the propaganda mill lets him know how lucky he is to have that generous retirement fund. He believes not a word of it.

He's not the only loser, however. To help make up the differential in pay, he runs a systems design and consulting business on the side, using the company's computer time, manpower, and facilities. Sometimes he evaluates proposed company projects as "not feasible" because of insufficient computer availability and manpower.

Another dismal disincentive is to toss your star performer a bone when he merits a bonus. A bright young executive was employed as assistant general manager of a chemical products company's Southeastern division. One day his boss suffered a heart attack. During his six-month absence the assistant came through like a pro. He assumed masterful control of the plant, worked fourteen hours a day, installed ingenious money-saving and money-making innovations—in short, he heroically brought the operation through the most trying time in its history. During that period the division more than held its own; it showed an outstanding profit. At year-end the assistant manager was rewarded with a $1,000 bonus and a letter of commendation from the president.

Seething, he was smart enough to realize that in view of the back-breaking six months he had put in and the results he had shown, the $1,000 was chicken feed. He also knew that with the president's letter of commendation and a dime he could make a local telephone call. Recognizing that his performance had attracted wide industry notice, he discreetly let it be known that he wouldn't be averse to a change should the right opportunity present itself. It did quickly enough. Today he runs his own operation and is proving to be a formidable competitor to his chintzy and insensitive former employer.

Nothing demotivates a manager faster than being made to feel that his fortunes are being controlled by a machine, however prodigious the gadget may be. In a large federal government agency "wage and salary review time" follows a long-established procedure that is pretty much in the hands of the computer. Under this evaluation-and-feedback system the unit chief sits at the head of a conference table, a computer print-out in front of him, and interviews his key people one at a time. The parade takes a full day to pass in review and follows an unwavering pattern. The manager enters the room on appointment and is nodded to a chair situated between his boss and the print-out. In the allotted time his past, present, and future are hashed over, with repeated reference made to the print-out. Inviolate, this can be neither contested nor denied. The computer rates individual performance on a scientifically graduated scale, and produces the hard facts to back up its rating.

After a harrowing session with this unwholesome twosome, a tight-lipped manager, with venom in his heart and resignation on his mind, confided, "There were times it wouldn't have surprised me had the boss addressed me by my employee number instead of my name."

Apt to be equally embittered is the victim of autocratic supercontrol. A savvy, experienced manager with a good track record was hired by the head of a medium-size textile products company to coordinate and supervise its marketing functions. He noted early in the game that for even relatively minor decisions, the chief's approval was required. It took little time for a confrontation to develop and even less time for the manager to conclude this was the wrong organization for him.

Conversely, when honest and realistic incentives are applied, the most remarkable gains are achievable: production records are broken, sales quotas exceeded, morale problems made to vanish.

In a nationally known manufacturer of airplane parts, heavy inventories were causing profits to drag. A variety of computer-based strategies were tried to help solve the problem. Nothing worked until the plant and product managers were put on an incentive program tied to inventory reductions. By cutting inventory they increased their income. The problem today is a thing of the past.

In a company that makes industrial flooring materials, for years sales compensation was geared primarily to the selling volume produced. If a salesman wrote a $10,000 order for material that yielded the company a 5 percent profit margin, he received pretty much the same commission he would get for a $10,000 order yielding a profit margin of 35 percent. When a new system was installed with sales commissions calculated to reflect margin of profitability achieved, the increase in corporate profits was spectacular.

The Eckerd drug store chain, according to one industry expert, has for years netted greater profits than most of its competitors largely because of what he describes as Jack Eckerd's motivational stress. One of a number of unique incentives Eckerd uses is to place big blocks of personally owned stock in a trust fund for employees at all levels and permit them to purchase the stock at a price substantially below market cost. This provides them with a practical means of participating in the enterprise. When people own part of the business, they have something to work for and protect.

Money may not be the only people motivator, but many realists believe it's still the strongest one around. Apart from the material things, money buys education and opportunity, peace of mind, dignity, and more. In large measure, if you know what to do with it, money buys happiness. Now add personal job satisfaction and fulfillment to good dollar incentives and you're playing ball with the pros.

"God made man to go by motives, and he will not go without them."

Henry Ward Beecher made this observation over a century ago, and it puts it all in a nutshell. Sure Fail management, when you boil it down, is little more than the failure to read and heed this advice.

CHAPTER 24

Untended Trends

Between now and the end of this century more new knowledge will be spilled out and recorded than in all previous history.

Organizations, willingly or not, are agents and vessels of change. Each of us, whether customer, client, proprietor, employee, or plain citizen, is caught up in its foment. Technology accelerates daily, and a mushrooming mass of products and procedures must face the challenge to keep pace. The demands of the marketplace change, along with the motivations that create the demands.

Alvin Toffler summed it up succinctly enough in his book *Future Shock:*

We are simultaneously experiencing a youth revolution, a sexual revolution, a racial revolution, a colonial revolution, an economic revolution, and the most rapid and deep-going technological revolution in history. . . . Each new machine or technique, in a sense, changes all existing machines and techniques, by permitting us to put them together into new combinations. The number of possible combinations rises exponentially as the number of new machines or techniques rises arithmetically. Indeed, each new combination may, itself, be regarded as a new supermachine.

149

Quoting social psychologist Warren Bennis, Toffler adds, "No exaggeration, no hyperbole, no outrage can realistically describe the extent and pace of change. . . . Only the exaggerations appear to be true."

Clearly there's a message here for the sand-burrowing executive. In the face of this mind-busting change myopic managers who remain stubbornly anchored to their swivel chairs will be in for a jolt that may shake their foundations. Trendonitis—the failure to heed and tend trends as they ought to be tended—is an affliction of the organizational muscles and joints that makes it painful to get your racket back and swing out at opportunities and problems. In today's fiercely competitive world if you don't swing out, you lose out.

One loser just a few years back was R. Hoe & Co., a New York producer of printing machinery. Touted as one of the hottest turnaround candidates of the late 1960s, the company bumbled its way into bankruptcy. It held a reputation for decades as a leading manufacturer of high-quality letterpress products. Trendonitis set in, however, coupled with a severe case of financial mismanagement. Although the industry was being swept by offset presses, Hoe refused to read or acknowledge the signs, lagging further and further behind competitors, until it became too late to make up for lost time.

Nor is it news to Autoland observers that in the late sixties Chrysler Corporation dug itself a deep hole because it turned blinders on the small-car trend. At a time when the market was hot for the trim Plymouth Valiant, the "big three" automaker locked itself into production on such high-profit gas gulpers as the Plymouth Fury, Dodge Polaris, and big-Chrysler models. It poured millions into big-car promotion while consumers yawned in response—the result: in a two-year period sales plunged almost 40 percent.

There are some watch industry watchers who feel that Timex Corp. got itself into a similar bind by waiting too long to move in response to the rapidly accelerating digital watch trend that started a few years ago. Now with the introduction of digital watches in the $20 to $30 range by such companies as Texas Instruments, National Semiconductor Corp., and Fairchild Camera & Instrument Corp., observers are waiting to see how large a chunk of Timex's mass consumer market the trend tenders can grab.

Trends represent opportunities for the sharp-eyed observer of business and life-styles and booby traps for intractable clingers to time-eroded tradition and custom. Clearly the need to get with it is most critical when trends begin to develop. It is at this point that organizational go-men run head on into conflict with organizational whoa-men. The go-man says "Now!"; the whoa-man says "Wait!". If the whoa-man's the head man, you wait.

Too often the problem is one of age and entrenchment. Never is the opportunity potential of a trend so exciting and clear as *after* it has just caught on fire. But by then it's usually too late to get started. By then the smart money is already invested, the wheels of production in motion. Joining a trend in its first-dawning stages can involve considerable risk, particularly in industries where heavy retooling is necessary. Will the trend continue and develop or fizzle and die?

The task of placing these considerations in proper perspective and balance can be an unappetizing diet to digest for a chief executive pushing retirement age. There he stands at the twilight of his career, admired, respected, awaiting his reward for a hard job well done. It's not easy for a man in his position to countenance a major upheaval. He knows who he is, where he's been, and where he's going. All he needs is to keep the boat on even keel for another year or two, and he's got it made. So he opts for delay, and Trendonitis sets in.

It set in around the early and mid-sixties when a large aerocompany failed to respond to indications of increasing market demand for commercial aircraft. While competitors, keeping close watch on indicators, tooled up for the expected order influx, this producer dug in and continued its focus on military contracts. When the trend's irreversibility became apparent, a massive program was kicked off to expand part-producing capacity and gear up for the change. But it took months to gain momentum, and precious headway was lost, along with several millions of dollars.

The unflappable whoa-man tends to wind up a woe-man in a wide variety of enterprises. Most chief executives try to glib their way out of trend-missing blunders via PR rationales that hoodwink none of the experts. A creditable handful possess the frankness and courage to own up to faulty decisions. One such man is Magnavox president Robert H. Platt (many years from retirement), who missed the trend from electron tubes to solid-state sets.

Back in the early seventies, when most TV makers were flopping over each other in the race to make the conversion, Platt decided to wait. He didn't think consumers would respond enthusiastically to the solid-state sets. What's more, he figured that in a year or two a better, brighter picture tube would be developed and wanted to wait for this before committing himself wholeheartedly to the changeover (if the trend picked up momentum).

It was bad judgment, he glumly concedes. "We didn't properly interpret the market trend, and as a consequence we got hurt badly in 1972."

Once the industry's most profitable TV manufacturer, according to *Business Week,* in 1972 Magnavox reported its lowest corporate earnings since 1964. Even more damaging are the ripples that can result from untended trends. In Magnavox's case many of its dealers turned to competitive lines to fill the void in solid-state sets.

Trendonitis is like a case of the flu. It can hit you when you're old and decrepit or you can be smitten when you're healthy, young, and in your prime. A case in point is Levi Strauss & Co. For a decade or more Levi was one of the staunchest, sturdiest, most profitable, dynamic, and social-minded corporations in America. Blessed with an enviable reputation for managerial prowess, the jeans maker was largely piloted by bright young executives, who chalked up a compound annual growth rate of 24 percent in a tough and competitive industry. Nonetheless, in 1973 it muffed an important trend, which seriously injured its prestige, turned a fat potential profit into a sickening loss, and disenchanted many fervent Levi loyalists in Europe, where corporate growth had been fastest.

In what is described by some as the company's most costly marketing blunder, it didn't respond with sufficient vigor to the bell-bottom craze that was sweeping through Britain, France, and points east. Despite warnings and pleas from retailers and distributors—accompanied by some threats to switch to local suppliers if Levi failed to deliver—the company neglected to come through. It shifted some of its U.S. and French production to bell-bottoms, but not nearly enough. In addition, it continued to overproduce straight-legs, long its primary profit maker.

True to retailer predictions, the demand for bell-bottoms multiplied as rapidly as the demand for straight-legs dwindled. In the end Levi was stuck with millions of pairs of the straight-legs in its European warehouses, many of which were sold at a loss. Instead of fat profits the company took a $12-million bath in the overseas market.

Untended trends are by no means confined to market trends that have been misread or ignored. As touched upon earlier, the past decade has seen the burgeoning of many other trends. One involves job enrichment, namely making work more meaningful and rewarding intellectually as well as financially. Organizations responding well to this trend attract superior job candidates and find it easier to retain top performers. Those that cling to outmoded apprenticeship and work control methods, where employees are treated like numbers instead of people, invite serious labor and quality problems.

In one New Jersey area where competition for qualified people is keen, a leading insurance company stubbornly refuses to acknowledge the job-enrichment trend, according to management consultant Leonard J. Smith. It keeps exceedingly close rein on employees, granting them little independence for creative expression and routinizing work to the maximum. As a result, says Smith, the caliber of its people—and service—has been steadily declining. Competitors recruit the bright young college graduates in the area and lure experienced and promising employees from the myopically managed firm.

Another key trend of the seventies, as we all know, is increasing corporate social awareness and responsibility. Powerful as this trend is, and inevitable as social restructuring appears, there are still many organizations bucking its progress and development. Some persist in countering social pressures with PR pronouncements designed to cool anger and hostility. As more and more visibility is being given to social irresponsibility, on the one hand, and see-through PR Bullshevism, on the other, corporate images are being undermined, recruitment efforts stymied, employee morale injured, and in an increasing number of instances sales performance pulled down.

How do you put an end to untended trends?

In some cases the answer lies in organizational restructuring, in constructive responses *built into the system.* This, as we have said, constitutes the cure for most major Blunderland bloopers. When a flexible system of industry and organizational performance indicators is established to flag deviations and changes as they occur, management, acting in concert, can work together to seize opportunities in time and attack problems before they can trigger a heavy loss or disaster.

The purpose of performance indicators is to inform management how key functions and programs are progressing. When a performance indicator "acts up," it is a warning signal. An integral part of the organization's information and communications system, it "rings a bell" for management, indicating that immediate action is needed. In industry, for example, performance indicators would flash a red alert when sales sagged below a predetermined level, when excess customer complaints were received, when too many employee grievances were filed, or when an undue number of product rejects were produced. In government, performance indicators would flash red when too many apartment buildings were abandoned by owners in a ghetto area, when the roll of welfare recipients started swelling, or when a middle-class exodus from an urban district occurred.

What performance indicators accomplish, in short, is to pinpoint key developing trends automatically and force timely management decisions in response to them as dictated, not by individual emotion or whim, but by organizational objectives and needs.

Acknowledgments

My thanks to many people including William Harrison Fetridge of The Dartnell Corporation, Philip Brass of Fabergé, Dick Conarroe of The Walden Company, Mike Dorota of Apex Electronics, Wilbur Cross of Continental Oil, Alden Todd of Haskins & Sells, Harold Wolfson of Rubenstein, Wolfson & Co., and others too numerous to mention for proving to me through personal experience that decent treatment and human concern creates in people the kind of response that inspires them to produce at their best;

To management consultant-educator Leonard J. Smith for his helpful insights into both people and enterprise; and

To David F. Linowes, the professional's professional, who so graciously gave of his time, wisdom, and counsel during this book's preparation, and to my editor, Howard Cady, who so perceptively pinpointed the book's organizational pitfalls, showed me how to avoid them, and provided invaluable writing assistance.